SAN JOAQUIN DELTA COLLEGE LIBRARY
D1034538

MODERN GLASS

FABER MONOGRAPHS ON GLASS

edited by R. J. Charleston

*

NINETEENTH CENTURY BRITISH GLASS

Hugh Wakefield

MODERN GLASS

Ada Polak

(*in preparation*)

ROMAN GLASS

D. B. Harden

EIGHTEENTH CENTURY ENGLISH GLASS

R. J. Charleston

BOHEMIAN GLASS

Karel Hetteš

VENETIAN GLASS

Paul Perrot

A. *Translucent vase with Japanese pattern, by Gallé*, c. 1889
Ht. 4½ *ins. Mrs Ada Polak, London*
(*See pages* 24, 85)

MODERN GLASS

by

ADA POLAK

NEW YORK: THOMAS YOSELOFF

First American Edition 1962
Published by Thomas Yoseloff
New York
Printed in Great Britain

To
MY MOTHER

CONTENTS

ILLUSTRATIONS

COLOUR PLATES

MONOCHROME PLATES

at the end of the book

FOREWORD

The past hundred years have witnessed developments in the art of glass which have no precedents in its previous history. Quite apart from the great technological improvements which have made possible the extensive use of glass in architecture, and for a hundred everyday articles into the making of which some element of art must enter, the period has been remarkable for the emergence of the designer who designs virtually for glass alone. After a period in which glass-makers had drawn, without full understanding, on the styles of the past, this new type of designer created glasses in the idiom of his own time, often contributing to the final development of that idiom by the style and beauty of the glasses which he designed.

The leaders of this first renaissance had frequently been schooled, like Gallé and Rousseau, in other branches of the applied arts, usually ceramics. Later, glass-designers were drawn from the ranks of painters and architects. Such were Marinot, Gate, Hald or Keith Murray. Today, the tendency is for designers to be trained from the outset for one specialized branch of industrial design. Each school has its own special strength and weakness, but there can be no question about the richness and beauty of the glass-tradition of the last century. Glass has become in a very special way the material which embodies *par excellence* the aspirations of modern design.

Ada Polak comes to the task of surveying this field with special qualifications and by specially favourable avenues of approach. The work for her great book on Norwegian glass of the eighteenth and early nineteenth centuries (*Gammelt Norsk Glass*) has given her an acute insight into the factors which go to the formation of glass style. Her years of work in the Museums of Norway, where nineteenth century art has always been studied with sympathetic interest, have developed in her an intuitive understanding of the art of the last hundred years. The present and the immediate past are always most difficult to see in their true perspective. Standards of judgment are not fully formed; sympathy and antipathy are undeservedly aroused. Whatever the caution necessary in making a final judgment, however, there can be no doubt at all of the skill and insight which Mrs. Polak has brought to the survey of her field. Her analysis of the developments in art glass during the past century, and her judgments on it, will command a universal respect.

R. J. CHARLESTON

ACKNOWLEDGEMENTS

The author wishes to express her grateful thanks to the artists and designers, collectors, museum curators and representatives of glass factories, who have kindly assisted in the preparation of this book by providing photographs of their glasses as well as much valuable information.

They are, in Austria: J. & L. Lobmeyr, Vienna; in Belgium: Cristalleries du Val-Saint-Lambert and Institut Royal du Patrimoine Artistique; in Denmark: Holmegaards Glasværk, Kastrup Glasværk, Mrs. Åse Voss Schrader and the Kunstindustrimuseum in Copenhagen; in Finland: The Finnish Society of Arts and Crafts, Helsinki; in France: Conservatoire National des Arts et Métiers, M. C. de Hauke, M. François Décorchement, M. Jean Sala, M. André Thuret, René Lalique & Cie., Musée des Arts Décoratifs, Musée Galliéra, and Syndicat Général des Cristalleries et Verreries d'Art, all Paris, and M. Maurice Marinot (†) and M. Pierre Levy (Photos M. Godin), in Troyes; in Germany: Gralglashütte, Landesgewerbemuseum and Miss Nora Ortlieb, both Stuttgart, Richard Süssmuth Glashütte, Staatliche Fachschule für Glasindustrie in Zwiesel and Württembergische Metallwarenfabrik; in Holland: N. V. Koninklijke Nederlandsche Glasfabriek, Leerdam; in Italy: Barovier & Toso, Seguso Vetri d'Arte and Paolo Venini (†), all Murano, and Dr. Astone Gasparetto, Venice; in Norway: Christiania Glasmagasin, Oslo, and the Kunstindustrimuseums in Oslo, Bergen and Trondheim; in Sweden: Gullaskrufs Glasbruk, Edward Hald, R.D.I., Kosta Glasbruk, Orrefors Glasbruk and Strömbergshyttan; in U.S.A.: The Corning Museum of Glass, Mr. Maurice Heaton, The Metropolitan Museum of Art and Steuben Glass, all New York; in Britain: Baroness Hermione Cederstrom, Mrs. Gabriella Gros, Mr. John Hutton, Mr. Keith Murray, A.R.I.B.A., R.D.I., Royal College of Art, Mr. Norman Sheldon, Victoria and Albert Museum, 'Vitrea' and Whitefriars Glass, all London; also Royal Scottish Museum and Mrs. Helen Monro Turner, Edinburgh, Foley College, Stourbridge, and Mr. Laurence Whistler, Dorset (Photo from *Engraved Glasses 1952–1958 by Laurence Whistler*, Rupert Hart-Davis, 1959).

The author would like to offer a special word of thanks to the Editor of this series, for his patient and untiring helpfulness in solving particular problems connected with the preparation of this book.

I

FIN-DE-SIECLE.

Art glass and colour-glass

A complete survey of glass in the modern world would fill a very large volume indeed. One major chapter would have to be devoted to plate glass and its manifold uses in building, transport and aeronautics, another to glass for radar, television and a great variety of scientific, optical and laboratory purposes. Modern lighting equipment made of glass would demand a broad treatment, as would bottles and containers, to say nothing of glass for kitchen and table use.

This book sets out to deal with one quantitatively very small branch of modern glassmaking – namely glass vessels where particular aesthetic qualities in the material, or decorative methods peculiar to glass, have been exploited with a genuine artistic purpose. Table-glass and other kinds of useful ware will be discussed only when necessary in the larger context; the main attention will be concentrated on what the French call '*vases de délectation*', and which we will call 'art glass'.

The modern conception of glass as a legitimate medium for the creative artist can be traced back to France in the latter part of the nineteenth century. At that time artists and designers in many Continental countries and in Britain felt the need for organized action to stimulate genuinely creative work in an increasingly industrialized society. The dependence of designers on historical models, which had been prevalent for more than a hundred years, was considered undignified and uncreative, while the discovery of Japanese art during the early 'sixties showed the way to new ideals of form and decoration as well as to a more ambitious attitude on the part of the artist towards the applied and industrial arts. Japonism[1] was

[1] For the terminology of styles of this period, see Stephan Tschudi Madsen, *Sources of Art Nouveau*, Oslo (1956).

the main inspiring force when in 1863 a French organization for the improvement of design was established by a group of '*artistes et fabriquants*' in Paris. Its final name became 'L'Union Centrale des Arts Décoratifs', and cardinal points of its programme were the founding of libraries and museums (Le Musée des Arts Décoratifs began its activities under its aegis in 1881), the publishing of a magazine (*La Revue des Arts Décoratifs* was first published in 1880), and, most important, the organization of regular exhibitions of contemporary work. It was at the exhibition of L'Union Centrale in 1878 that the two pioneers of a modern art of glass, Eugène Rousseau and Emile Gallé, first attracted serious attention. Their most important work was done in colour techniques, some of which were highly complicated. The basis for this sophisticated work with colour is to be found in the production of *opaline*,[1] which had taken place in France during the preceding decades.

Love of colour was of course inherent in the Romantic Age, and it can be seen reflected in most products of the time. At the beginning of the nineteenth century colour in glass was something new. From *c.* 1680 to 1825 transparent, colourless glass with engraved and cut decorations had been the main product of makers of fine glass in most parts of Europe. During the neoclassical period towards the end of the eighteenth century, opaque-white glass, occasionally tinted to a cool blue, had been fashionable, but deeper explorations into the possibilities of coloured glass did not really begin until the eighteen-twenties. It seems that the Bohemians were the first to experiment seriously with colour in glass. Their 'hyalith' and 'lithyalin' glasses, which imitated precious stones, were invented during the 'twenties, and so was their flashed and cased glass with patterns cut through the coloured surface down to the colourless base. A few years later the Venetians began to look to their own great past in glassmaking. The old colour techniques of *millefiori* (with sections of rod in different colours embedded in the glass), *latticino* (with opaque-white threads in fine patterns worked into clear glass), and *aventurine* (with spangles of metallic particles integrated into the substance of the glass) had brought glory and riches to the glassmakers in Murano during the Renaissance and Baroque periods. About 1830 they were revived in Murano itself in an antiquarian spirit, and soon a taste for elaborate Venetian colour-glass spread to other European countries. During the 'thirties, and with Bohemia and Venice as their models, French glassmakers began to produce colour-glass, which was of a finer technical and artistic quality than that

[1] *Opaline* is a modern collector's word to describe the coloured art glass, mostly made on a slightly opacified basis, in mid-nineteenth-century France.

made anywhere else. The decisive personality during the early years was Georges Bontemps (1799–1884), the technical leader of the factory of Choisy-le-Roi in Paris from 1823 to 1848. In 1839 he began to produce *latticino* glass in the Venetian style, while cased glass in the Bohemian manner was made by him from 1842 and *millefiori* from 1844 onwards. Other factories soon followed suit, Clichy, Baccarat and Saint-Louis being the most important. French colour-glass was shown at frequent exhibitions in France and abroad, and the factories vied with each other in showing a succession of new and exciting colours. In form their products were at first traditional. Bohemian and Venetian glass was copied, and classical ceramic forms were also used as models; sometimes details from different sources were combined in a single piece. Later, free furnace-worked shapes were developed, and moulding came into general use. If extrinsic decoration was used at all, it was applied by free-lance craftsmen working in private studios in Paris. By the middle of the century, French colour-glass had become famous for its originality, grace and elegance, and for the first time in history France came to the front rank among the glass-making nations of the world.

It was on the technical foundations laid down in different French factories between 1840 and 1860, that Rousseau and Gallé, with their more conscious artistry and consistent ideas of style, created a modern art of glass.

E. Rousseau

Eugène Rousseau (1827–91) began as a 'faïencier' or designer of and dealer in decorative faïence in Paris. In 1867 he began to take an interest in glass. At first he merely made designs for glass models, but soon he entered into a close partnership with Appert Frères, an enterprising firm at Clichy. The exact character of the collaboration is not known, but the glasses which carry Rousseau's name show that he must have penetrated deeply into the technicalities both of the making and decorating of glass. His display at the Paris Exhibition in 1878 greatly impressed the critics, and at the Exhibition of 1884 his glass was greeted with unreserved praise and much enthusiasm for its beauty and originality. The following year he gave up working in glass.

Not many of Rousseau's glasses can be identified today, and their exact chronology cannot be reconstructed. The following survey of his work is based on small groups of his works in museums in Paris and London.

The impact of Japanese art on Rousseau is mentioned by one of the critics in 1878, and it is easily recognized in existing pieces. Japanese pottery has obviously provided the models for certain vases with simple outlines, surface effects resembling running glazes and decorations of Oriental figures and landscapes cut into casings or flashings of coloured glass (Plate 1). The metal in these, as in most of Rousseau's glasses, is transparent with a soft, yellowish hue, and is best described as champagne-coloured. Rousseau's Japanese pastiches show that he had grasped, not only the obvious elements of the Oriental style – the asymmetrical composition, the lyrical landscapes, the figures in Japanese costume – but that he had absorbed the Japanese message in its subtler aspects. The shapes of his glasses are based on simple geometrical forms, the lines are drawn without sharpness or rigidity, and the decorative details are executed with loving care.

Rousseau employed a great variety of decorative methods with the finest skill and taste. The Bamboo Vase, acquired by Le Musée des Arts Décoratifs in 1878 (Plate 3), shows a rich combination of varied techniques. The swelling middle section is decorated with enamelled flower patterns, which shine in brilliant blues, whites and gold, while the square form of the main body with its softly rounded corners has a finely cut and polished pattern of bamboo leaves. A vase of thinly blown glass is covered with a fine pattern of flowers and leaves painted in gold, contrasting with a boldly drawn pattern of chrysanthemum (Plate 2). Engraving is employed in a peacock pattern on a tall covered beaker (Plate 18). The metal is of the usual champagne colour; the shape is based on the medieval German type of 'Humpen'; the cut pattern is simple and executed with much subtlety, so that all is softness and grace.

But Rousseau's most original contribution to the art of glass was provided by his vases with effects of colour and texture inlaid in the glass itself. By applying different metal oxides to glass, which he afterwards covered with a transparent casing, he obtained embedded, flame-like streaks; the texture could be further varied and enriched by the addition of metal particles or by crackled effects (Plates 4, 5). Contemporary critics compared Rousseau's glass to precious stones, and it was admired not only for its beauty, but for its novelty. Nobody since the Venetians of the sixteenth century had played so cleverly with colour in glass, and as the effects were used in a massive material instead of the brittle Venetian *cristallo*, completely new aesthetic effects were revealed. Rousseau applied his colour technique to objects of very large size, the shapes of which were borrowed from varied historical sources, German (Plate 4) or Italian Renaissance (Plate 5) or Oriental art. Some of them were mounted in metal. Most of his models seem to have been reproduced in several copies

(Plate 2). The generous size of his vessels, their simplicity of outline, boldness of colour and rich succulence of material all contribute to make his art a truly monumental one. In spite of the exquisite character of Rousseau's glass, it never becomes precious.

Rousseau's career as a glass artist was short and his output small. In its day it was known only to a handful of amateurs in Paris and to specially interested visitors to the Paris Exhibitions. His colour-glass was tentatively imitated both in France and in Britain, but it never became a popular genre. When Rousseau himself withdrew from glassmaking, his pupil and assistant E. Léveillé carried on his work. Glass from the firm of Léveillé-Rousseau is much better known. At the Paris Exhibition of 1900, Léveillé's glass attained great popularity and samples of his work were acquired by museums and private collectors in many countries. With their soft colour-streaks and crackled effects they are very handsome, even if they lack the grandeur of form and richness of material of the real Rousseau pieces. An individual contribution by Léveillé to the style established by Rousseau is the use of relief or even free sculptured effects, mostly in the form of deep cutting or furnace-worked ribbings and convolutions (Plates 7A, 7B).

Two other of Rousseau's assistants did work of independent character. During the 'nineties A. G. Reyen produced some pretty, if somewhat insipid, cased-glass vases decorated with flowers and butterflies, and E. Michel, who had worked as engraver for Rousseau and Léveillé, began about the turn of the century to make crackled colour-glass in fanciful shapes in the style of the time (Plate 29).

E. Gallé

Emile Gallé (1846–1904) was the only son of a producer of luxury goods in Nancy. Decorated faïence and high-class furniture were the chief lines of Charles Gallé's firm; with his wife he inherited a mirror factory, to which he himself added the production of table-glass. Emile Gallé learned the glassmaker's trade at Meisenthal, a factory on the Franco-German border with a certain reputation for its decorative glass, and at the art school in Weimar he received a more formal art education, which was completed by studies in the museums in London and Paris. In 1865 he designed crystalware for his father's table-glass factory, and he also collaborated with him in the faïence production. In 1867 he established his own workshop for glass decoration, and in 1874 the two Gallé's began regular production of art glass in Nancy.

At the Exhibition in Paris in 1878 Gallé established a reputation as an inventive and original glass artist. He showed opaque, coloured and marbled glass, as well as triple-cased glass with gold leaf inserted between the layers and enamel-painting on the surface. His display at the Exhibition in 1884 showed further variations on these and other themes, and Le Musée des Arts Décoratifs acquired several pieces. They are mostly of transparent glass, decorated with enamelling, cutting and engraving. Ornaments are freely borrowed, but never slavishly copied, from varied historical sources: medieval church art, heraldry, Chinese export porcelain, seventeenth-century rock-crystal and eighteenth-century Bohemian and Silesian glass. Sometimes different decorative techniques are combined in a single piece in an almost confusing variety: the form of the 'porte-cigare' in Plate 8B is inspired by Chinese pottery, the cut decoration is naturalistic, while the dark red colour-streaks must have been derived from Rousseau's glass. The technical quality is of the very highest, and there is a youthful freshness and exuberance about the whole collection which is very charming indeed. Ornamental lettering, which later became such an important feature in Gallé's glass, appears sporadically.

The 1889 Exhibition in Paris is usually considered Gallé's finest hour, and a large group of his glass was again acquired by Le Musée des Arts Décoratifs. They are mostly coloured in the mass, with cutting and engraving used as auxiliaries to the furnace-work. The cased-glass technique has been widely employed. In the vase with the blue casing (Plate 11B) it has been used in heraldic simplicity, while the famous 'Orpheus Vase' shows it in its greatest complexity, with layers of glass in many different colours and shades cut away into figures; the technique is, however, not the natural one for the rendering of the complicated figure subject in the grand classical style. The decoration for the 'Orpheus Vase' was designed for Gallé by the painter Victor Prouvé from Nancy, Gallé's friend and associate all through his active life.

But the most important novelties in the 1889 collection are the exercises in Japonism with flowers and insects as main decorative motifs (Plate 9B and Colour plate A). Here the colours have taken on a new softness, and a fresh note of grace and lyricism has been introduced. Picturesque titles or long literary quotations, suggesting the theme of the decoration, are written on the side of many of the vessels, and most of them are conspicuously signed with Gallé's name.

The years between 1884 and 1889 must have been formative for Gallé. The restless searching among all manner of historical styles, which is characteristic of his 1884 collection, seems to have come to an end in 1889, and a consistent mood of poetic gentleness and grace is prevalent. The decisive factor in his development seems to have been Japanese art. In

Paris, the Japanese fashion had begun in the late 'sixties, and Gallé must have been acquainted with the style long before 1889; it is possible that he had occasion to absorb the Japanese way of thinking more intimately in 1885, when a Japanese artist paid a prolonged visit to Nancy. However it all happened, it is obvious that in 1889 Gallé's talents had been canalized and directed along new paths, which he was to follow with ever greater concentration. As early as in 1884 he writes in his *Notice d'Exposition* that 'la nature est toujours prise . . . comme point de départ', but it must have been after the 1889 Exhibition that he developed to maturity that 'nature-style', which was to epitomize so many of his thoughts and ideas, and to bring him his greatest fame.

Gallé's love of flowers and trees was more than the artist's affection for a pretty motif. All his life he was a practising gardener and a learned writer on horticulture, and every flower and leaf to be seen in his decorations can be identified as belonging to a real botanical species. In his choice of motifs he did not limit himself to fashionable lilies, orchids and seaweeds or the fruit blossom made popular by the Japanese, but used sturdy homely plants like the thistle and the oak. In his writings he never tired of expressing his fondness for the flora of his home country, Lorraine in the Franco-German border-region, and his patriotic sentiments must have been further strengthened by the political events of 1870–1. Gallé's love and understanding of flowers, which is one of the most genuine features in his complex personality, gave freshness and vitality to his conception of the Japanese style, and it became the central point in that philosophy of art which he developed during the early 'nineties.

To Gallé as to Ruskin nature is the source of all beauty, as well as the inexhaustible treasure-house for the artist in search of living form and ornamental motifs. Nature is interpreted as that idyllic section of it where flowers bloom, insects hum and birds flutter in the trees, which was also the inspiration of the Japanese artists, and which Gallé himself knew so intimately and loved so well. The essence of all art, whatever the medium in which the artist finds expression, is poetic thought and emotion—hence Gallé's '*verreries parlantes*' (according to his *Notice d'Exposition* of 1884 first launched that year), where a quotation from some great poet, written on the glass, has inspired its form and decoration. Sometimes the quotations are borrowed from Lorraine writers or from the great national poets, but frequently they are taken from the writings of the Symbolists, from whose theories so many elements in Gallé's philosophy are inspired. Underlying all Gallé's writings and artistic production is the idea, which is the essence of Symbolism, that art should not describe or state but suggest and evoke. But the final aim is a moral one: art should '*adoucir les hommes*'.

With his own deep love of nature as the mainspring, stimulated by the Japanese fashion, influenced by contemporary discussions on art in Britain and France as well as by the work of fellow-artists in Paris, Gallé created about 1890 his own version of the *Art Nouveau*, the poetic style of decoration which emerged in France about 1889–90 and which was the first conscious and collected effort by the artists of industrialized Europe to create an original and truly contemporary style. The fact that Gallé's glasses were the first of their kind to express the fashionable style of the time gave them an exciting air of novelty, which to some extent accounts for their great popularity. Through his writings in contemporary periodicals Gallé spread the gospel of his faith; his enthusiastic and extrovert personality easily gained proselytes; the example of his tremendous business success, as a glassmaker, a producer of decorative faïence and of inlaid furniture with *Art Nouveau* ornaments, must also have won him many followers. In Nancy he became a real *maître d'école* who in the most direct manner stimulated a number of manufacturers of luxury goods to adopt his own graceful version of the *Art Nouveau.*

These widely varied activities did, however, distract him from that close personal attention to the production in his glass factory on which his early fame had been based. In his own writings we can follow how his establishment developed from a personal studio to a big industrial concern. In 1884 he describes how he has begun to take in pupils, who work as designers and decorators under his directions. In 1889 a decorators' studio has been established, where wooden moulds are made for the use of the glass-blowers, designs for ornaments are painted in water-colour, and a great selection of 'nature vivante et morte' is at the artist's disposal in the garden and the natural history collection annexed to the works. 'Mon œuvre personelle', he goes on to say, 'consiste à rêver pour le cristal des rôles tendres et terribles. . . . j'impose par avance, autant que je puis, à la matière ondoyante et diverse, les qualités qu'il me convient qu'elle ait, elle et ses colorations, ses arrangements, pour incarner mon rêve, mon dessin.' In other words, Gallé had become the head of a large organization of artists and craftsmen who worked to his will. His own inventive powers, on which the whole activity rested, began to show signs of strain. During the 'nineties he went on launching new colours of ever greater subtlety and with increasingly picturesque names: 'bleu céleste', 'bleu troublé' and 'crystal améthyste à couche neigeuse' were among the novelties of 1892. To obtain greater variety he began to add foreign materials to his glass, such as semiprecious stones and seashells. The famous 'La Libellule' (Plate 8A) is a striking example of Gallé's personal style in his later years. It is an exercise in Japonism. From the eggshell-smooth ground with its shimmer of blue-grey-mauve shades the body of the dragonfly stands out in sharply contrasting colours and very high relief; part of its body is actually lifted from the background. The rim of the bowl is softly undulating, while the foot has no other purpose than to carry all this loveliness. It gives intense expression to Gallé's lyricism, and technically it is incredibly clever, but the effect is more of porcelain than of glass.

Side by side with the making of these very complicated unique pieces, each of which must have been fruits of Gallé's personal inventiveness and technical skill, went the production of vast numbers of vases large and small, mostly 'natural' and asymmetrical in shape, and decorated with clinging flowers and plants. Most of them are made in the cased-glass technique, and the genre must have been directly derived from a type of glass vases, made in China during the latter part of the eighteenth century, with flowers in relief cut out of a coloured casing on a milky background. A similar technique can be seen on some Chinese snuff-bottles from the same period. Gallé developed the style with the subtlest understanding of the transparency of each colour and its capacity for blending with its neighbours. One fine example of many is the Oak Vase in the Victoria and Albert Museum (Plate 10) with its simple shape, suggesting the sturdiness of the oak tree, and its handsome decorative design of leaves and acorns in the finest shades of green, yellow and brown, varied with oxidized colour-streaks. The majority of Gallé's cased-glass vases were, however, made with a simple relief in one colour – a heavy mauve is particularly favoured – on an opaque white background, frequently tinted with 'waves' of colours. This genre, which can suitably be described as 'standard Gallé', must have been established during the early 'nineties to answer the growing demands for Gallé's glass, and it must to a large extent have been produced by his staff (Plate 11A).

During the 'nineties Gallé's fame increased rapidly. About 1900 he employed about three hundred people in his factory, and salerooms for his goods had been opened in several foreign cities. His stand at the Exhibition in Paris in 1900 was the sensation in the French section, and the show was spectacular, not to say theatrical, with a working furnace in the centre having an inscription from Hesiod over the glory-hole, and showcases grouped around it with heavily decorated vases displayed among living flowers and costly materials. Gallé himself was awarded a Grand Prix, and four of his assistants, Albert Daigueperce, Emile Munier, Julien

Roiseux and Paul Oldenbach, received silver medals. The great public was delighted, but the more discerning critics were less enthusiastic. Jens Thiis, a young Norwegian museum director and an ardent champion of modern style, wrote on his return from Paris: 'Gallé has lately worked under the increasing pressure of demands for ever more expensive glass, and under the growing responsibility which his great name as an artist lays upon him. It is always difficult for an artist successfully to reconcile these two consequences of world fame. This collection from the famous workshops in Nancy undeniably shows some unevenness in artistic quality. Emile Gallé, who originally created his art glass with his own hands and who expended so much love and imagination and idealistic thought on every one of them, is now working at the head of a large staff of technicians, whose help he must rely on to satisfy the increasing demands for his famous products. The collection in Paris was large and impressive, but less genuine and personal than his exhibition in 1889.'

From Gallé's death in 1904 and until 1913 the factory continued art glass production in Gallé's style with Victor Prouvé as art director. The firm seems to have carried on for some time after the war, and it is certainly a fact that 'Établissements Gallé' exhibited in Paris in 1925, but the firm's later history is obscure.

In an extensive material of Gallé's glass it has been possible on one occasion only to find two identical pieces (Plate 12) and it may be that by varying and interchanging shapes and ornaments, colours and techniques, he really did manage to keep up a production of unique pieces by the hundred and thousand within the fairly narrow stylistic idiom he had created. The same ornaments in identical colours were certainly repeated on pieces of varying form (Plates 12, 13). Most of his glass was very expensive to make. But in his *Notice* to the Exhibition in 1889 Gallé refers to his cheap production: 'Neither I nor my workmen have found it impossible to reconcile cheap production with art. . . . I have avoided all that is false, misshapen or brittle, and I have used colours that endure.'

Gallé's production of art glass can be conveniently divided into four main groups.

First there are his unique pieces up to 1889, which must have been very numerous in relation to his whole output during that period. Most of the existing examples are of clear glass with enamelled decoration, and they are mostly charming works of a highly personal character (Plate 9B). Secondly, the great number of cased-glass vases with a decoration of flowers and leaves, the majority of which must date from after 1890. Many of them are subtle in design, rich in colour and technically highly complicated; these may to a large extent have been designed by Gallé himself (Plate 10), while the very large group of 'standard Gallé' with conventional *Art Nouveau* flower patterns in one colour against an opaque white background (Plate 11A) must to a large extent be factory products. The boundary between the two classes within this second group is not always distinct. Thirdly comes the large and varied group of vases in serial production, where shapes, ornaments and colours have been repeated, though in so many different combinations that it is extremely rare to find two pieces that are exactly alike (Plates 12, 13). Finally there are Gallé's personal experimental pieces from after 1889, exaltedly lyrical in feeling and of the highest technical complexity (Plate 8A). In spite of their tense emotional atmosphere and over-elaborate character, they must be put *hors concours* with any other type of glass; they are true landmarks in the history of art glass.

It should also be mentioned that Gallé's factory produced table-glass. The types that can now be identified are 'rustic' in shape and without external decoration, and wonderfully intimate and free from pomposity as compared with the over-ornate table-glass which was in the highest fashion at the time.

It is difficult to try and arrive at a final appreciation of Gallé as a glass artist. His personality was made up of so many different and conflicting elements – real artistic talent, enthusiastic idealism, showmanship and a shrewd sense of business – that it is hard to define the genuine core; while the output of his factory was so vast and so varied as to make a general survey of its production an almost impossible task. The opinions of his own contemporaries about him were nearly without exception over-enthusiastic and uncritical, while writers of the following generation were correspondingly negative and derogatory. Detailed research into his biography, the history of his factory and its products is badly needed.

Compared to Rousseau, with his fine sensitivity and balanced sophistication, Gallé can seem naïve, pretentious and even vulgar. But it is of course in his very extravagance that his greatest charm and attraction lies, and to our own generation, with its romantic leanings, Gallé's exuberant lyricism – if such an expression may be permitted – has a genuine appeal.

Always very beautiful are his pictures of flowers, leaves and insects. They have preserved the character and charm of their models in nature, and through careful stylization they have also become graceful ornaments. In Gallé's personal pieces the colours are subtle and imaginative, and in the best cased-glass pieces the relief is full and generous. But in the more routine examples style has sometimes become mannerism, the flowers droop and the colours are sickly and sharp. Form was undoubtedly less important to Gallé than colour and ornament, and the shapes of his glass have sometimes been criticized for a lack of constructive feeling. This is valid in the case of some of his 'natural' shapes, which imitate trees, rocks and shells, but in such cases shape is so much of a piece with the ornamentation that we accept it all as contributing to one integral unity. It should also be remembered that there are plenty of plain and 'constructive' shapes among Gallé's glass, especially in his early period. The criticism which is sometimes levelled against Gallé's glass for being 'unglassy' is perhaps more legitimate.

Gallé's most spectacular contribution to the style of his time, indeed to the history of styles, is that pretty nature-style which he developed soon after 1889. It became the accepted idiom of 'L'École de Nancy', and it also represented an important aspect of the *Art Nouveau* within the greater international context. This style, we must believe, was first developed in glass, as so many of its peculiar features – the fluid mobility of line, the subtlety of colour – seem directly inspired by glass. Gallé knew glass more intimately than any of the other materials he worked in; it represented his earliest experience with art and design, and his pre-1889 glass can hardly be called 'unglassy'. But during the 'nineties, when this style was applied with equal facility to glass, faïence and inlaid furniture, the original harmony between style and material was disturbed. Seeing himself as the prophet of a creed, and looking on his materials as a means of preaching it, he did in many instances try and make glass do more than it is capable of – express a view of life or carry a philosophical message – and the simple and fundamental qualities of the material became obscured by technical tricks and meaningful decoration.

Frequently 'unglassy' and unattractive is the opaque-white base to the coloured reliefs in 'standard Gallé'. In a large industrial establishment it must have been a necessity to have a neutral material in constant production to provide backgrounds to the many-coloured decorations on the cased-glass vases, but Gallé's opaque-white glass, whether it remains white or has 'waves' of colour, is heavy, dry and characterless, and it compares unfavourably with the smooth milky white material in the Chinese cased-glass vases which must have been his direct models.

But whatever individual opinion may be of Gallé's glass, in the history of art glass he undoubtedly occupies an exceptional position. His factory's output of unique pieces must have been quantitatively greater than that of any other glassworks before or since, and no single person can at any time have mastered such a wide range of techniques for the making of fine glass: the chemistry of colour-glass, furnace work, moulding, the use of oxides and metals, enamel-painting, cutting, wheel-engraving and acid-etching, he knew them all and used, changed and combined them to suit his own needs. And, perhaps most important of all, through the popularity and fame of his glass and through his own enthusiastic propaganda for glass as art, he gave a new status to glass in the minds of public and artists alike. To this end the signing of his glass was of immense importance. It is a simple psychological fact that the collector likes to be able to attach a name to his treasure, and the consistent and conspicuous signatures on all Gallé's glass, especially after a certain date (probably 1889), gave his glass the character of 'real' art and added enormously to his fame. Contemporary glassmakers and followers took up the habit, and while before Gallé signed glass is rare, on modern glass signatures have become almost the rule.

Gallé's glass was eagerly copied inside and outside France during his lifetime and after. Closest to Gallé's own products were those of the firm of Daum in Nancy. It was founded by Jean Daum in 1875 with a group of Alsatian craftsmen, most of them originally ceramic workers. In 1890 Jean Daum's sons, Auguste and Antonin, came under the personal and direct influence of Gallé, and began to make glass decorated with flowers and leaves in cased glass or other furnace techniques (Plate 9A). Some of the early *Art Nouveau* glass from Daum is very fine, but production went on until the First World War, and the later examples are of little artistic interest. Like so many products by the adherents of 'L'École de Nancy', Daum's glass lost its tension when Gallé's inciting personality was gone. Cased glass in a style similar to Gallé's was also made at Sèvres to the designs of the firm of Landier & Fils, and at the factory of Lunéville, near Nancy. After 1900 the Belgian factory of Val-Saint-Lambert made some respectable glass in the style and technique of 'standard Gallé'. For the Swedish factory of Kosta, the painter Gunnar Gunnarson Wennerberg designed cased-glass vases in Gallé's manner between 1898 and 1903; some of them were shown in Paris in 1900. Some fine pieces in Gallé's manner were executed by A. E. Boman at the factory of Reijmyre to the designs of Ferdinand Boberg. In 1911 Boman produced about a hundred pieces of cased-glass vases in a similar, but rather crude, style at Hadeland in Norway.

French studio work

While the new art of glassmaking made spectacular progress in the factories of Clichy and Nancy, 'les recherches délicates' into the artistic potentialities of glass were being carried on in a number of small studios in Paris.

The exquisite pastiches of enamel-painted Islamic glass of Joseph Brocard had first attracted the attention of critics at the World Exhibition in Paris in 1867, and given them the first hope of a renaissance in the art of glass. Later, perhaps stimulated by the activities of Rousseau and Gallé, Brocard produced some enamelled glass in a more independent style (Plate 14). A pair of bowls in Le Musée des Art Décoratifs in Paris (Plates 15A, 15B) are decorated with simple flowers and leaves. They are cool in colour and composed in a formal rhythm which recalls Islamic decoration, and seem extraordinarily modern for 1885. The form of the glass and the painted decoration are closely integrated: the leaves have first been moulded on the side of the vessel itself and then picked out in enamels. In pieces like these, Brocard must have collaborated very closely with the makers of his glass.

At the Paris Exhibition in 1878 A. Jean showed some iridescent glass with engraved or enamelled flowers which was highly praised by the critics. A few examples of his glass were acquired by the Conservatoire National des Arts et Métiers in Paris, where they can still be seen. Some pieces in coloured glass with painted and gilt decoration are of admirable quality, but truly astounding is the large vase on three feet made of transparent glass with 'waves', freely formed at the furnace, round the middle (Plate 6). Here Jean has taken up problems of glass aesthetics which have not been studied seriously until recent times, and solved by none so boldly and satisfyingly.

Jean was primarily a potter, and we know that both Rousseau and Gallé worked with ceramics as well as with glass. The two arts could of course most fruitfully be carried on together. Many aesthetic problems were common to both materials, and so were a number of decorative techniques, such as painting and gilding. Perhaps it was the fact that the young French art of glass was grafted on to the nation's solid old ceramic tradition, that gave it its astounding technical quality and surprising air of sophistication right from the first. The close connection between glass and ceramics in these early stages may also to some extent account for the predilection for solid material effects which is a general feature in French glass during the late nineteenth century. At this time one can almost speak of a ceramic style of glass.

Pâte de verre

Halfway to pottery were the artists who worked in *pâte de verre*, a plastic material of powdered glass, which can be made into sculptural forms or vessels by a process of moulding. The technique, which was known in antiquity, was revived in modern times by the Frenchman Henri Cros (1840–1907). Experimenting in a furnace at the Sèvres factory, he managed after many years of research to find a composition of powdered glass which could be coloured and moulded. Between 1893 and 1903 he produced his famous series of reliefs in several colours, some of which can now be seen in Le Musée des Arts Décoratifs in Paris. A potter at the Sèvres factory, Albert Dammouse (1848–1926) began experimenting with small vessels in *pâte de verre* in 1898. His material was a soft enamel paste somewhere between soft porcelain and glass. This slightly translucent material he moulded into fragile vessels with delicate flowers in pastel shades: of all *pâte de verre* products the vases of Dammouse show perhaps the finest harmony between form and material (Plate 16). At the Exhibition in Paris in 1900 Georges Despret (1862–1952) showed some small bowls in 'natural' shapes of a heavier *pâte de verre* in dark shades. François Décorchemont was originally a painter and potter; from 1904 he dedicated himself completely to the making of vessels in *pâte de verre*; until 1914 he made small vessels decorated with animal or plant motifs in *Art Nouveau* style (Plate 17). Gallé also occasionally made *pâte de verre*.

Britain and the Continent

About 1880 the firm of James Powell & Sons (Whitefriars) in London began to produce some exquisite glass in a thin metal with light bowls on slim and elegant stems, and with combed colour-inlay in a style derived from Venice. The style, which was invented by Harry J. Powell (1853–1922), has a distinct flavour of the Arts and Crafts Movement and the *Art Nouveau*. This and other manifestations of the style of the time in English glass have been fully discussed by Mr. Hugh Wakefield in the companion volume to this book, devoted to *Nineteenth Century British Glass*.

Between 1892 and 1900 the painter and etcher Karl Koepping in Berlin (1848–1914) designed some tall attenuated goblets and decanters in various colours, which were produced from tube-glass. The flower on its stalk was the starting point for the shapes, which were *Art Nouveau* to an exaggerated degree, and the colours were subtle and exotic – one contemporary critic even describes them as wicked and morbid. Koepping's glass became popular and examples were acquired by several museums, but a contemporary French writer calls them 'amusette', and today they are mostly interesting as period pieces. Glass in a similar style was made at about the same time by the glassblower Friedrich Zitzmann in Wiesbaden.

L. C. Tiffany

The only glass artist of the period to approach the popularity of Gallé was the American, Louis Comfort Tiffany (1848–1933). He was born in New York, the son of a dealer in jewellery, antiques and modern applied art. The firm had branches in Paris and London and workshops in other European cities, and was at all times in the closest touch with trends of fashion on both sides of the Atlantic. Tiffany began his career as a painter. After some years of training in the studio of George Innes, he studied in Paris, travelled widely in Europe and the Near East, and rapidly established himself as a successful painter of landscape and genre in a tentatively Impressionist style. In 1876 he showed some pictures at the Philadelphia Centennial Exhibition. Here he became struck with the contemporary decorative arts and particularly with the Japanese products, which were also exhibited, and from that time he turned all his attention to the applied arts.

His first ambition was to make stained-glass windows as he had seen them in the French cathedrals, made as mosaics of glass coloured in the mass, and put together in a framework of lead, and he began studying the technique and chemistry of glassmaking in the Heidt factory in Brooklyn. In 1878 he established his own glasshouse in New York with the Italian Andrea Boldini in charge, but as this and a subsequent factory both burned down he returned to Heidt. It was in order to utilize the left-overs from his window-glass production that Tiffany turned his attention to blown glass. At first he tried to fashion his coloured glass into naturalistic flowers, which he embedded into the thick bases of clear glass vessels, while other scraps of coloured glass were made into jewellery or small boxes mounted in metal.

In 1889 Tiffany visited Europe, and it is legitimate to assume that he visited Paris, and that it was Gallé's startling display at the World Exhibition in that year which caused him to revise his ideas about how to make use of coloured glass. In 1892 he reorganized his firm as the 'Tiffany Glass and Decorating Company', and by the following year his glass factory, the 'Tiffany Furnaces' at Corona, Long Island, was in operation. Here he surrounded himself with a team of expert glassblowers, and began serious experiments with coloured and iridescent glass for blowing. He was not himself a practising glassmaker, but with his intimate knowledge of many sides of the industry he could direct his staff very closely, and the production became a very personal one. In the manner of Gallé he began creating his own colour effects, which he gave picturesque names like 'Mazarin blue', 'Samian red' and 'Blue green satin of the peacock pattern'.

The first collection of Tiffany's blown glass was exhibited at the Columbian Exposition in Chicago in 1893, and it became an immediate popular success. His vessels were fascinating novelties, which caught the style of the time and answered to the now general demand for subtle and exquisite effects, and the output of the factory was increased and the styles varied. In 1900 he reorganized his firm as 'Tiffany Studios', under which name it worked until 1936. By this time Tiffany's art glass had become famous among collectors on both sides of the Atlantic, and at the 1900 Exhibition in Paris it was almost as popular as Gallé's. Today it can be studied in a great number of examples both in Europe and the U.S.A.

Tiffany's glass vessels are usually blown thin and are light in weight. Occasionally the shapes are inspired from the Near or Far East, but otherwise historical derivations are rare. The majority of his products are permeated by a genuine *Art Nouveau* feeling. Some forms suggest flowers on stems (Plate 20), others have indents and protuberances that make them look like trunks or branches of trees, whilst yet others have the simple outlines of Japanese pottery (Plate 19B). They are all made in coloured glass in a great variety of shades, many of them very deep and dark. Through clever furnace work the colours have been combined into fluid line-patterns (Plate 21A). Tiffany did really exploit to the full the material's 'artistic suggestiveness and the readiness with which it combines with itself, color with color and glass over glass', to quote from a booklet which was published by the firm in 1896. Here it is also described how some of his glass is decorated by 'carving, by cutting through one layer of glass down to one of another color', i.e. he also worked in the cased-glass technique. In the catalogue prepared for the Paris Exhibition in 1900 it is proudly declared that 'in none of the specimens of this glass is there any application of decoration by painting. Such designs as are found are in all cases produced by the combination of different colored glass during the operation of blowing the piece'. With all the right in the world could Tiffany advertise his blown glass as 'favrile', a word which denoted 'made by hand' in old-world language, and whose sound suggested the elusiveness that his glass tried to evoke. He used the word to describe all his glass products, stained glass, mosaic and plaques as well as blown glass.

In the catalogue for the Paris Exhibition in 1900 it is stated that 'in common with most artistic natures . . . Mr. Tiffany loses much of his interest in an achievement as soon as it deserves that name. This . . . results in an almost bewildering variety of effects'. Between 1896 and 1900 ideas for blown glass seem to have flown incessantly from his mind. Favourite decorative patterns were peacock feathers (Plate 20), one of the most typical motifs of the *Art Nouveau*, and big round leaves reminiscent of Japanese ornamentation (Plate 19A). Flowers and twigs are sometimes suggested both in shapes and surface decorations, but a majority of the tooled patterns of his glasses are purely abstract compositions of flowing lines (Plate 21A), which divide and converge in elegant *Art Nouveau* rhythms.

But what most of all gives to Tiffany's blown glass its distinctive character is the shimmering metallic iridescence of the surface. He must have experimented with the technique in connection with his stained-glass windows and mosaics as early as 1880, for in that year he applied for patents for metallic iridescence. The effect had been used on glass in the Near East in medieval times, but during the 'seventies it had a new vogue in Europe: iridescent glass was made by Lobmeyr of Vienna and by Thomas Webb at Stourbridge, while at the Exhibition in Philadelphia in 1876 iridescent glass of fine quality was shown by American makers and favourably commented on. According to Tiffany himself, the direct inspiration for his use of the technique was the iridescence on excavated Roman glass, which he is said to have seen for the first time in Paris in 1889. In the booklet from 1896 already quoted, the iridescence of his glass is described as having been achieved 'by a careful study of the natural decay of glass and by checking this process, by reversing the action in such a way as to arrive at this effect without disintegration'. Close observation of ancient glass, the description continues, reveals the process of disintegration in stages, 'how sections like of pearl or of onion appear on the surface, and how, when two of these meet, like the rings round two knots of wood, the curves of decomposition unite and form sinuous lines.' No wonder this was inspiring to an *Art Nouveau* artist. A more technical description of the process of producing iridescent effects is found in the catalogue for the Paris Exhibition in 1900: 'If it is desired to make use of metallic or iridescent lustre the still hot article is subjected to the fumes of metals reduced to a state of vapour, and these being absorbed by the glass in a succession of thin, delicate films, so refract the light, resolving it into its constituent colors (exactly on the same principle as the nacreous layers in a shell) that the rainbowlike play of colour is obtained.' 'There will always be,' he adds, 'one or two (pieces) which, by the happy accident of favouring conditions, are far more perfect than all their fellows.' This can easily be observed in existing glasses. On some the iridescence adds a real poetic quality to the general effect, but sometimes the lustre lies like a covering glaze over the surface, giving a matted and slightly rough texture, which is not altogether pleasing. If the iridescence is very thick, the impression is of metal rather than of glass.

Until soon after 1900 blown glass seems to have been Tiffany's chief interest, but at that time the most creative phase of his career as a maker of glass vessels had come to an end. The style of *Art Nouveau,* which had inspired him to his finest exploits in blown glass, was going out of fashion, and his artistic ambition took other directions. The factory went on making blown glass until after the First World War, much of it in the fashion established before the turn of the century, but other kinds of glass were also made: in a catalogue from 1908 the factory is described as producing cameo glass and clear crystal with carved reliefs. As time went on the stress was laid increasingly on useful goods, especially lamps. This is not the place to discuss Tiffany in all his other capacities, as a maker of stained-glass windows, pottery, metalwork and jewellery, as an interior decorator and a benefactor to young artists. In the history of art, it is perhaps as a maker of fine glass vessels in the style of the *Art Nouveau* that he will be chiefly remembered.

Critics of the period were apt to discuss Gallé and Tiffany as parallel phenomena, and even today a comparison may be fruitful. Tiffany was not, like Gallé, instrumental in creating the style of his day. He seems to have taken over the *Art Nouveau* at the very moment of its inception, and to have given it a very personal interpretation. Perhaps he had a more balanced feeling for form, colour and decoration than Gallé; his technical imagination was, on the other hand, more limited. Sometimes, when Tiffany goes outside the stylistic idiom of his own period, his glass looks astoundingly modern (Plate 21B).

Tiffany's glass was widely copied on both sides of the Atlantic. In 1898 the Bohemian firm of J. Lötz Witwe at the factory of Klostermühle took out a patent for a process of making iridescence on glass which was very close to Tiffany's own, and Klostermühle's style of form and decoration are also largely derived from Tiffany's. Several other factories in Bohemia are mentioned by Pazaurek as showing iridescent glass at the Paris Exhibition in 1900. A detailed list of Tiffany's imitators in America is given by Larry Freeman (see Bibliography).

2

FUNCTIONALISM: 1915-1940

The new style

The taste for coloured, furnace-worked art glass in a poetic *Art Nouveau* style, which had been established by Gallé and Tiffany between 1890 and 1900, remained unchallenged until the First World War. It was the impact of Functionalism on the applied arts during and immediately after the war which changed the picture.

The new style, whose roots modern historians have been able to trace far back into the nineteenth century, first emerged in its mature form in architecture between 1900 and 1914. Its main principle, that function should determine form, is of course not a new one. Both as a theory and as a basis for practical solutions in architecture and the applied arts, it is as old as history. The early twentieth-century architects, like H. Berlage in Holland, Walter Gropius and the Bauhaus group in Germany and Le Corbusier in France, did however set out to realize it with a more relentless logic and more scientifically detached minds than anyone before them, and by applying their principles to the special needs of the modern age, and by availing themselves to the full of the many new materials and methods now at their disposal, they really did create something new. The early Functionalist buildings were works of pure engineering, construction and material were all, and the general effect was simple to the point of harshness; the stress was on the technical, economic and social problems connected with production and building. Its early champions professed to be unconcerned with appearances; what was perfectly suited to its purpose would be beautiful by itself. Very soon Functionalism did however develop its own aesthetic code; its chief creator was perhaps Le Corbusier. Form should be simple, outlines clean and straight and surfaces plain; the 'honest' use of the materials most suitable for the particular purpose would produce textural effects so significant and so satisfying in themselves, that ornamentation in the traditional sense would be superfluous. If ornament were to be used at all, it should be based on 'absolute' geometric relationships. Functionalist aesthetics were influenced by Cubist painting, and just as the classical ideals of proportion and composition can be clearly distinguished behind the abstract forms of Cubist art, so early Functionalist architecture and design were based on classical ideas of formal relationships; at the same time the formal conceptions revealed in primitive art were having an increasing impact on the aesthetic ideas of painters and sculptors, architects and designers.

Functional art glass is a contradiction in terms, but Functionalist aesthetics became the most important influence on art glass between the wars. The impact on glass was demonstrated in a sensational way at the Exhibition in Paris in 1925, especially in the collections from France itself, from Italy, Sweden and Holland. The dusky lyricism of the *Art Nouveau* had given place to an astringently rational and sophisticated mood. Cool transparent glass in simple basic forms was generally favoured, while ornament was sparingly used, and disciplined and formalized to the highest degree. The will to be modern, to forget the past and start afresh in a brave new world was felt by all.

The different national versions of the modern style in glass, which were first shown in an international context in Paris in 1925, had largely emerged independently of each other in the various countries. Until the outbreak of the Second World War glassmakers in Europe and America went on working on the lines first laid down between 1915 and 1925.

ARTISTRY IN FRANCE

M. Marinot

The greatest and most decisive personality in the history of art glass between the wars was Maurice Marinot (1882–1960). He began as a painter, and together with his friends Derain, Villon and Segonzac he became one of the leaders of the school of Fauvism. Between 1905 and 1914 he exhibited regularly at the Salon d'Automne and the Salon des Indépendants. Most of his paintings from this early period were destroyed by German bombs in 1944, but a 'Mother and Child', which was acquired by Le Musée de l'Art Moderne in 1951, shows a preference for a clear and orderly composition and an audacious and imaginative use of colour. Marinot's interest in glass began in 1911, when he visited the glass factory of his friends the brothers Viard at Bar-sur-Seine, near his home town of Troyes. He began to design and direct the production of glass, which he afterwards decorated with enamels. Glasses in this genre were first shown at the Salon des Indépendants in 1912; they were simple in shape, and decorated with heads and figures of women in a mondaine Paris style (Plate 23), and they became collectors' objects from the very first. Marinot pursued the art of enamelling until about 1922. As his understanding of the technique increased, the decorations became ever richer in colour and texture, and in the not very numerous pieces he made after the First World War, the designs are drawn with wonderful freedom and refinement, and the colours are of the greatest subtlety. There is, however, a youthful zest about the pre-war pieces which gives them a special attraction.

Meanwhile Marinot had become increasingly interested in the material of glass itself and the methods of working it, and one of the glassblowers at the factory taught him the elements of his craft. From this basic knowledge he began exploring the artistic possibilities of glass and the glassmaker's tools, proceeding slowly and laboriously along the narrow path of trial and error. 'Tout ce que j'ai fait, j'ai fait difficilement,' is one of his succinctly formulated sayings, which in quick glimpses seem to illuminate important secrets of his art. At the furnace he worked alone or with a boy to help him with the heaviest manipulations. The personal work with the material was of essential importance to him. Ideas born during the work at the furnace were developed at the drawing board, and finally the mature idea was realized in intense and purposeful concentration before the glory-hole. 'C'est chaque fois une belle bataille, un plaisir profond dans l'effort physique.'

All through his career as a glassmaker Marinot favoured a heavy massive material, which he formed into vessels with simple, smooth outlines. In 1922 he began using the technique of acid-etching in a highly personal way. The process had been taken up by French glass technicians in the middle of the nineteenth century. Gallé discussed the method in the *Notice* for the Exhibition in 1889, and said it will not do for delicate work, but 'it cuts into certain glasses in a manner of its own', and from 1890 onwards he did use it quite extensively in his factory. Marinot took up acid-etching because it served his purpose better than any other method. His vases and flacons in this technique are of massive, transparent glass, occasionally tinted, and the etched designs, some of which form intricate abstract patterns of a highly intellectual nature, are slashed deeply into the surface and give a semi-sculptural effect (Plate 24A). Every inch of the surface has

B. *Flacons with inlaid colours, by Marinot*
M. C. de Hauke, Paris
(*See page* 41)

been under treatment, and the most varied textural effects have been obtained (Plate 22). To Marinot the technique was certainly no short-cut to easy decorative work. He sometimes had a single vase in hand for a year before the complicated ornamentation in reliefs of varying depths and in different planes on the surface was complete.

Marinot's most exclusive contribution to the art of glass was, however, made in pure furnace work. From about 1922 and until the end of his career as a glassmaker, he blew all his glass personally, and he himself considered the work in this genre as the most important he had done, especially what was undertaken after 1927.

Marinot's *travail à chaud* proceeded along two main lines. On the one hand he worked with inlays of colours, sandwiched between thick layers of transparent glass (Plate 25B and Colour plate B). The colours were made by the application of various metal oxides to the core of the glass in a technique related to that used by Rousseau. Impressions of bark, moss or running water, gathered on his country walks, furnished ideas for colours and textures, and in order to obtain the exact effect he had in mind, he worked out the chemistry of each one himself. On the other hand, he embedded clouds of air-bubbles in the thick walls of the glass to obtain foamy effects. Glass in this style was occasionally tinted, a soft greyish yellow being a favourite shade (Plates 24B, 25A).

From very early in his career Marinot had admirers who eagerly bought his glass. The Galerie Hébrard in Rue Royale was his Paris agent. At the Exhibition in Paris in 1925 Marinot's glass became known to a wider public, and during the years that followed it was exhibited all over the world, and he was loaded with honours of every kind. In 1934 a film was made showing him at work at the furnace. During these years he continued with unswerving integrity to penetrate ever deeper into the secrets of his material. His last show was at the Exhibition in Paris in 1937, where he was *hors concours* at the prizegiving. Soon after he had to give up glass-making. The physical effort of manipulating the heavy vessels in the glare of intense light and heat from the furnace had affected his health, and after twenty-seven years of complete and uninterrupted concentration on glass, he returned to his painting. All his glass is now in private or public collections. In England it has not been possible to trace a single piece.

The utilitarian principles of Functionalism were of course foreign to Marinot. He has said himself that the mere thought that his glass should have any useful purpose would distract his concentration and inhibit his creative powers. The simple, uncluttered forms which allow the spectator to take them in at a single glance are, however, derived directly from the aesthetic code of Functionalism, and so is the primitive, rough and even brutal quality which can be detected in some of his acid-engraved pieces. Even more profoundly inspired by Functionalism is his determination to let form grow naturally from the material and the process, which is the main underlying principle of all his work *à chaud*. In a conversation with Guillaume Janneau he has given expression to his intense experience of the basic qualities of glass and glassmaking in simple words: 'In the chief part of every vessel there should be the appearance of swelling, which is the characteristic evidence of blowing. It is this which best expresses the method by which the glass was formed, and which gives the fullest effect to its brilliance with the varying sheen of light on its bulging sides.' Marinot was aware of the great stylistic movement of his time in its most profound aspects.

Marinot brought to glass the great talent and deep artistic consciousness of a French painter, trained in one of the most stimulating *milieux* in the history of European art – Paris during the first decade of the twentieth century. He was privileged to work under the most favourable conditions imaginable, exempt from all commercial considerations and with complete freedom to pursue his artistic ideas. The result is an *œuvre* where every piece bears witness to the maker's deep intimacy with and understanding of the material, and which in sheer beauty stands in a class by itself.

Marinot's glass became widely influential, especially after the Exhibition in Paris in 1925, when his style was a sensational novelty. The simple and natural economy of his glass was something startling at a time when most glassmakers who wanted to be 'modern' were still struggling with the superficial characteristics of Functionalism. Marinot was the first to exploit to the full the aesthetic possibilities of heavy, massive glass, and in this he not only inspired serious glass artists in his own and other countries, but he created a broad and popular fashion, which has been exploited by commercial firms all over Europe in ashtrays and vases of crude colours inlaid with regiments of air bubbles. His acid-etched glass was also copied and vulgarized. Well could the Président du Syndicat des Verriers Français introduce him at the opening of the glass exhibition in Le Musée des Arts Décoratifs in 1951 with the words: 'Marinot, à qui vous devez tout.'

A group of French glass artists are direct followers of Marinot on a high artistic level.

About 1930, Georges Dumoulin, originally a potter who had worked for the Sèvres factory, produced a series of highly finished vessels of simple forms and massive material with inlaid effects reminiscent of slate and marble. On the occasion of the Exhibition in Paris in 1925 the sculptor Henri Navarre (b. 1885) began to make furnace-worked glass and glass with foamy inlaid effects, mostly in sombre colours (Plate 26B), and he did some interesting work during the 'thirties. His early glass was made by the firm of UMAD, his later by La Verrerie de la Plaine St. Denis, near Paris. Navarre has also produced some pure glass sculpture, which is technically highly impressive. André Thuret (b. 1898) began making glass in 1924. He is a professional glass technician, and like Marinot he makes all his glass single-handed. His work between the wars was produced at the factory of Alfortville, near Paris, on a basis of slightly tinted transparent glass, from which he produced some fine pieces *à chaud* (Plate 27B). Mention should also be made of Aristide Colotte, originally an engraver, who made some elaborate sculptured pieces by a special method of cutting and polishing.

French studio work

Jean Sala (b. 1895) is the son of Dominique Sala, a Spanish glassmaker who settled in Paris in 1910 and made a name for himself as a glass artist; Jean Sala was his pupil and close follower. Until a few years ago he worked in a studio workshop on the Left Bank in Paris, where he mixed his batch, founded his glass, blew it and decorated it at the furnace single-handed. He worked in a lightweight metal, tinted greenish blue and by incomplete heating made purposely *malfin*, full of bubbles and imperfections; in appearance it is not unlike some ancient Roman glass. This he formed with nimble hands into vessels of gay, simple shapes, based on rough sketches made beforehand; the immediate inspiration while working at the furnace often made him change his first projects. When he wanted decoration, this was also applied at the furnace in the form of melted glass in contrasting colours (Plate 27A). The attraction of his work lies in its grace and spontaneity. He and his father sometimes made figures in the virtuoso Venetian style; the collection of glass fish made for the aquarium at Monaco is famous.

Between the wars Décorchemont continued to work in *pâte de verre*, as the only one of his generation. He worked in a fairly heavy material, reminiscent of natural stone in consistency and colouring, which he moulded into plain shapes, at times somewhat hard and angular in outlines (Plate 28A). In later years he has done some exquisite sculptural work, which both in material and shapes is reminiscent of jade (Plate 28B).

Jean Luce (b. 1895) designed engraved, cut and enamelled decoration for glass and pottery in a fashionable and somewhat superficial modernistic style. Marcel Goupy (b. 1886) designed and decorated some very tasteful glass between 1918 and 1936. For many years he was head of the decoration department of Rouard, the dealer in luxury glass and ceramics in L'Avenue de l'Opéra. Founded at the beginning of the century the firm has sold glass by Navarre, Thuret, Décorchemont, and has undoubtedly been a stimulating factor in the development of French art glass.

French factories

About 1920 the firm of Daum in Nancy finally discarded the cased-glass style in Gallé's manner which had been its chief artistic language for more than a generation (apart from some pretty enamelled glass made between 1910 and 1915). In their search for a modern idiom in art glass, the leaders of Daum looked to Marinot. A vase of transparent blue glass, made for the Paris Exhibition in 1925 (Plate 26A), is technically much simpler than anything Marinot ever did, but in its neat, closed outlines and rough textural effect it is reminiscent of his glass. Daum also took up acid-etching, but used the technique in a much less powerful way than Marinot.

The only concession to modernity by the factory of Baccarat at the Paris Exhibition in 1925 was the introduction into its traditional cut-glass style of 'cubistic' motifs of squares, circles and triangles.

Much more independent was the work done by René Lalique (1860–1945). Lalique first became famous at the Paris Exhibition in 1900 as a designer of jewellery in an exquisite *Art Nouveau* style. His combs, brooches and pendants from that period relied largely for their beauty on inlaid coloured glass pastes. At the same time he experimented with glass for vessels and for decorative window-panels. A commission from the perfume manufacturer Coty for a series of luxury flacons gave both encouragement and direction to his efforts, and in 1908 he acquired a small glass factory of his own. He experimented for some time with blown glass. Some of his vessels from the years before the First World War show running glaze effects, reminiscent of Japanese pottery, but they are more robust and straightforward in shape than the fashionable *Art Nouveau* glass. Unfortunately, very little seems to have survived of Lalique's blown glass production, which is today best studied in the periodicals of the time.

In 1918 Lalique acquired the factory at Wingen-sur-Moder near the German border, where all his glass has since been made. Here he developed that genre of glass which has chiefly become connected with his name: vases, flacons, bowls and jars, decorated with ornaments in relief produced by a process of moulding, and mostly made of colourless glass with a frosted surface. 'Lalique's glass has the ethereal brilliance of Arctic ice,' said his great admirer Guillaume Janneau in 1931. When colour is used, it has in most cases been applied afterwards, and striking colour contrasts, with sealing-wax red or shiny black against white are preferred (Plates 30B, 31B). Occasionally he used subtler colours, produced in the furnace, and some of his glass has an opalescent sheen (Plate 31A). Among the decorative motifs the female figure recurs frequently, both as relief or in free sculptural form, while birds, fish and flowers are other favourites. Lalique's use of animal or floral subjects for his decoration is far removed from Gallé's lyrical naturalism. Lalique always submits his motif to the severest laws of pattern-making: birds march in friezes in quick, nervous rhythms (Plate 30B); branches and leaves or parrots in a tree make a regular network of lines enclosing the whole vessel; fishes play in symmetrical pairs. Purely abstract patterns are also used, as in a vase with a bold arabesque in very high relief picked out in shiny black, made for the Exhibition in Paris in 1925 (Plate 31B).

During the 'twenties, his most creative period, Lalique also produced some vessels of a more ambitious character, vases and cups of large dimensions and with decorations in the grand classical manner, which reflect his innate feeling for monumental effects (Plate 30A). While most of his glass was turned out from the power-press by the dozen or the hundred, some of these larger vessels had to be made singly by the *cire perdue* process. He also used glass in an imaginative way for fashionable interior decoration on a larger scale, in clocks and chandeliers, decorated mirrors and fountains.

In its hard worldliness, Lalique's glass caught the mood of the 'twenties to perfection, and his works formed a natural setting to the world of fashion, where girls shingled their hair, smoked cigarettes in long holders and danced the one-step and the Charleston. The style lingered on into the 'thirties, but in the later models it has lost much of its verve.

SENSE AND SENSIBILITY IN SWEDEN

Sweden's great contribution to modern design was to transform Functionalism from an intellectual theory into a practical instrument for better living. The style created by the Swedes on the basis of the social and aesthetic ideas of the great reformers, first in the applied and industrial arts, later also in architecture, has to a large extent become accepted as practical and pleasing by ordinary people all over the Western World.

Glass was only one of the materials of the applied arts to which the Swedes brought freshness and originality under the aegis of Functionalism. But whereas fitness for practical purpose, toughness in wear and cheapness of production were prime considerations in so many of their early Functionalist products, their glassmakers aimed from the very beginning at making precious products of sheer beauty. In no other branch of modern design have the Swedes revealed such rich artistry as in their glass.

To understand the authority and sophistication of Sweden's modern architecture and design, it is useful to remember that the country, which today has become a model democratic state, has a very strong aristocratic tradition. Since the seventeenth century, when Sweden was a major political power in Europe, there has been a fastidious public for art products of high quality. During the reign of Gustavus III (1771–92) – the greatest royal mæcenas in a long line of art-loving kings – a preference was established for the classical ideals of restraint, balance and simplicity. These have since become traditional elements of Swedish taste. In 1845 the Svenska Slöjdföreningen (the Swedish Society of Industrial Design) was founded for the encouragement of national crafts. It was one of the first organizations of its kind in Europe, and theoretical discussions of questions of art and style have been matters of general public interest ever since.

Before 1930

During the First World War the acute housing-shortage and the lack of raw materials for household goods created a new and urgent interest in the problems of production and style. Functionalism seemed to provide the perfect programme for the austerity production necessitated by the war, and its doctrine was preached by theorists and widely accepted by designers and producers. Svenska Slöjdföreningen, remodelled and brought up to date, became the efficient organizing force behind the campaign for good design in mass-produced articles. In 1915 the slogan 'Handsome Household Wares' was launched to stimulate the new Functionalist manufacture, and another, 'Let the Artist design for Industry', followed as a natural consequence. Many Swedish factories responded and engaged artists to direct their production. Most important for the history of art glass were the appointments in 1916 and 1917 respectively of Simon Gate and Edward Hald, both painters, as designers to the glassworks at Orrefors.

Orrefors is situated in the heart of Småland, the main glass-producing district in Sweden. The oldest glass factory in the area is Kosta, founded in 1742 and still one of the major Småland works. Since its foundation, more than a hundred smaller factories have branched off from Kosta and from each other; today there are about thirty-five of them. Most of the Småland glassworks have been small in size and short-lived, but the continuous activity in glassmaking in the area has established a solid local tradition of craftsmanship and a real *milieu* from which more ambitious achievements could grow. In the eighteenth century there was an iron foundry at Orrefors. Glassmaking was taken up in 1898 with inkwells and table-glass of the simplest kind as the main products. But when in 1913 the factory was acquired by Johan Ekman, he and his enterprising manager, Albert Ahlin, determined to try and extend the repertoire of their products to include decorative glass.

Simon Gate (1883–1945) and Edward Hald (b. 1883) were contemporaries, but in social background as well as in personal character they were very different. Gate was the son of a prosperous farmer, and had been trained as an artist in the grand classical manner at the Academy in Stockholm; by temperament he was romantic, emotional and gifted with a real sense of drama. Hald was born and bred in Stockholm, and had learnt to paint in Matisse's studio in Paris; crisply intelligent and with a sophisticated sense of humour, he is essentially an urban type. Before he came to Orrefors Hald had designed pottery for the factory of Rörstrand, whereas Gate was new to industrial design. They both had to learn about glass and glassmaking from the most elementary beginnings, and in Knut Bergqvist, master glassblower at the factory from 1914, they found not only a first-class craftsman but a man of invention and original ideas.

The earliest Functionalist designs by Gate and Hald to be realized were some cheap services of table-glass, which were produced at Sandviken, Orrefors's daughter-factory for utilitarian ware, the first of them dating from 1917. Some of them are very 'natural' and 'rustic', and hark back to Gallé and the 'nineties, but a few are simple and severe – truly Functionalist creations.

But for the more ambitious products at Orrefors, Functionalism did not at first provide guiding principles. The earliest fruits of Gate's experiments with glass are some tall, thin vases in tinted glass with a touch of classicism (two handles at the sides) and a flavour of *Art Nouveau* in the exaggerated slimness of the shapes. They are mainly interesting today because they show Gate's first intense experience of glass and glassblowing. The earliest experiments of Edvin Ollers, who worked at Kosta about the same time, are closely related to these earliest efforts of Gate's. A more mature example of Simon Gate's art in pure glassblower's style is the graceful goblet with a leaf round the stem from 1923 (Plate 34), while a vase from 1930 with a black foot and rim is a heavier, but equally genuine expression of the fluidity of glass (Plate 35).

But what the director and manager at Orrefors had had specially in mind when they engaged the two artists, was that they might be able to improve on the factory's production of cased-glass vases, carried on in the manner of Gallé since 1914. In 1915, while Gate's engagement at Orrefors was being negotiated, Ahlin wrote: 'We make coloured art glass in a technique like that of the French glass artist Gallé, that is, with two or three casings in different colours. The decorative patterns are etched out of these, until one gets the desired coloured effect. Some artists from the Academy have given suggestions for designs, but . . . we shall be lucky if half of them can possibly be produced. Now I would like to know if Gate would be interested in making us some suggestions.' Before this, Ahlin and Bergqvist had been speculating about 'how to get rid of those sharp reliefs on Gallé's glasses'. During the year 1916 Ahlin, Bergqvist and Gate between them worked out their improvements on the Gallé type of cased glass. The new technique they arrived at was proudly called 'Graal glass', and it became the starting point for the Orrefors production of colour-glass, the factory's finest and most original contribution to the modern art of glass.

In Gallé's cased glass the process of cutting and etching the ornamental pattern from the casings was of primary artistic importance, and the finished vessels were essentially products of the decorators' workshop. In the production of Graal glass, the cutting of the pattern into the layers of the casings marks an intermediate stage in a much longer process, and Graal glass is given its final form in the furnace, where the ornaments acquire that fluidity and essential 'glassiness' which constitute their greatest fascination. The earliest Graal glass is a vase which both in shape and decoration is very close to Gallé (Plate 32), only the smoother surface and greater mobility of pattern distinguish it as a piece of Graal. In the period that followed Gallé was left far behind, and the personalities of Gate and Hald came strongly into evidence. Gate favoured decorations in many colours with figures in vivid movement (Plate 36), while Hald, who started designing for Graal as soon as he arrived in 1917, preferred light and elegant line-patterns (Plate 37). Most of Hald's later works in this technique are of a purely ornamental character, and are beautifully restrained and dignified (Plate 40).

But it was the engraved glass from Orrefors which won the factory its earliest international fame, and which became the basis for its extensive export production. An engravers' shop was already part of the factory's equipment, with Gustaf Abels at its head, and Gate and Hald began experimenting with the technique as soon as they were settled in. The stylistic background for the early Orrefors engraving was that elegant neoclassicism which was the fashionable style for luxury products of every kind in prosperous post-war Stockholm; its greatest and most famous monument is the Stockholm Town Hall by Ragnar Östberg, completed in 1923. Within this accepted stylistic framework, the two artists created each his individual style. Gate designed heavy vessels of large dimensions, deeply carved with figure subjects from the Bible, classical mythology and other august sources (Plate 41). Hald preferred a more brittle material with shallow engraving, decorated with subjects in a lighter vein, like 'Fireworks' (Plate 39) and 'Girls playing ball' (Plate 33); the latter is directly inspired by the art of his one-time teacher, Matisse. Sometimes he wittily exploits the transparency of his material. Engraved glass from Orrefors soon became the rage in Stockholm, and at the Paris Exhibition in 1925 it had a resounding international success.

During his early years as glass designer, Gate experimented with cutting, and some of his results are extremely fine, but he did not pursue his successes, the technique probably being too limited for his exuberant imagination. Hald never designed much for cutting. The most interesting early Swedish contributions to cut glass came from Kosta, where Ewald Dahlskog (from 1926 to 1929) and Elis Bergh (from 1927 until recently) made some very fine things (Plates 76B, 38). Bergh's artistic personality seems to have found its most complete expression in this technique. His cut-glass models are beautifully restrained and unfussy. He favours softly undulating lines, and the brilliance of the glass is never allowed to be hard and exaggerated.

After 1930

In Swedish design the Exhibition in Stockholm in 1930 marks the dividing line between tentative and mature Functionalism. On that occasion the new style was launched with a flourish in architecture, and afterwards it became the accepted style also in the applied arts, even for the most expensive luxury goods. In glass, the graceful elegance of the neoclassicism from the 'twenties gave place to a powerful and robust style with massive three-dimensional effects and simple, closed outlines. The influence of Marinot, whose glass Gate and Hald had had occasion to study in Paris in 1925, can be traced in some vases and flacons of simple, unified shapes, made in glass of one colour, and dating from 1930. The production of Graal glass was also renewed. In the early versions the metal had been fairly light and thin, but after 1930 the technique was employed in heavy, massive vases, where the ornaments are deeply embedded in thick casings of clear glass (Plate 40). Graal was now frequently combined with the 'Ariel' technique, which was invented about the interesting year of 1930. It has been described at Orrefors as 'organized air-bubbles', and consists of patterns, sandblasted into the core of the glass, which, when the casing is laid over, form enclosed channels of air where the patterns have been cut away. The initial process can be varied and developed and combined with colour-inlays. Hald has worked in Ariel, and so have Vicke Lindstrand (b. 1904), who was attached to Orrefors 1928–41, and Edvin Öhrström (b. 1906), a sculptor who has been on the permanent staff at Orrefors since 1936. Lindstrand's 'Penguins' from 1938 (Plate 45), and Öhrström's primitive abstractions from 1939 (Plate 44) with their shining, gliding figures in deep, glowing colours seen through the thick casing of transparent glass, are among the most powerful creations of Orrefors, and among the purest works of art glass ever conceived.

In engraving, deeper relief on heavier material came into favour. A fine example of Gate's style of the 'thirties is his 'Queen of Sheba' from 1938 (Plate 42). Generally speaking, the engraved ornamentation became simpler and the motifs more firmly organized and concentrated on the surface. A striking example of this development is Lindstrand's 'Shark-killer' from 1937 (Plate 43), a real Orrefors classic.

The example of Orrefors stimulated many Swedish factories to take up the production of art glass with professional designers to direct it. The work of Edvin Ollers, Ewald Dahlskog and Elis Bergh at Kosta has already been mentioned. Hugo Gehlin designed for Gullaskruf from 1930, and Monica Bratt for Reijmyre from 1937, and both have produced some very tasteful, if technically fairly simple models. Many other designers at other Swedish factories during the period could be mentioned.

In a class by himself stands Edvard Strömberg (1872–1946), a glass technician by profession. From 1917–18 he was attached to Kosta; between 1918 and 1928 he was technical director at Orrefors, and with his profound knowledge and understanding of his material he helped more than any other single person to create the technical conditions necessary for the artistic expansion of Swedish art glass. From 1928 he and his wife, Gerda Strömberg, directed the production of sober cut glass at the Eda works. In 1933 he founded his own small factory in the heart of the Småland forest, and the last years of his life were dedicated to the production of glass in the purest of styles. Strömberg never made coloured glass – it was the limpid transparency of crystal that fascinated him. The metal he made was pleasantly firm, though soft in consistency, and gently toned towards grey, mauve or a very pale blue, and its beauties were brought out in all their subtleties in the pure and sober forms designed by his wife, where the curve of a line or the gently increasing or decreasing thickness of material can suddenly reveal the finest shades of texture and tone (Plate 76A). Like the glass of Marinot, that of the Strömbergs is essentially of its period, but in its basic simplicity of a timeless and absolute beauty.

IN SWEDEN'S FOOTSTEPS

Denmark

Functionalism had had a great impact on Danish architecture and design before the First World War, and during the years immediately after the war, artists working for the Copenhagen porcelain factory had started experimenting with designs for modern table-glass at Holmegaard, at the time Denmark's only factory for such ware. With the appointment to Holmegaard in 1925 of the architect Jacob E. Bang (b. 1899), a more ambitious production of glass began. Without launching into complicated technical experiments, Bang applied his sound architectural feeling to the construction, not only of table-glass, but of vases and bowls decorated with simple engraved linear patterns (Plate 47B), with acid-etched ornaments or rough surfaces in the genre of Marinot, though very much simpler in design and technique. Straightforward, pleasant and charming, Jacob Bang's glass for Holmegaard during the 'twenties and 'thirties is a typical, if not spectacular, manifestation of good Danish design in a Functionalist idiom.

Norway

In 1928 Sverre Pettersen (1884–1959) was engaged as designer to Hadelands Glassverk, at the time the only factory for table-glass and decorative glass in Norway. A designer of textiles, stained glass and book-bindings as well as of glass, he made some excellent tableware for Hadeland, and also designed for engraving. A main line over many years was provided by goblets and vases with personal symbols and allusions, engraved for individual customers in a neat and graphic manner. He also did some free figure compositions in a style close to Edward Hald's. During the 'thirties he did some very interesting pieces with sandblasted decoration in a heavier style (Plate 46B). From 1937 onwards, tbe sculptor Ståle Kyllingstad (b. 1903) designed heavy, engraved vases for Hadeland.

Finland

The making of art glass in Finland was first taken up in 1928, when Henry Ericsson (1898–1933) became artistic adviser to the factory of Riihimäki. During the 'thirties Arttu Brummer (1891–1951), who was Director of the Central School of Arts and Crafts in Helsinki, also designed for the factory. The engraved glass of Orrefors was the main source of inspiration, and some very tasteful things were made in this idiom. A gentle style in blown glass was also favoured (Plate 46A). Compared with the independent and original Finnish architecture and pottery of the time, however, the Finnish art glass of the 'thirties seems somewhat tame. Of great interest therefore is a production of vases in plain, often green, glass, made in 1938 at the factory at Karhula-Iittala to the designs of the architect Alvar Aalto (Plate 47A). In line and rhythm they are strongly reminiscent of the bent-wood furniture which Aalto produced at the time, and which created a sensation by its bold modernity and unorthodox production methods. With its loose, asymmetrical rhythms and extreme technical simplicity, Aalto's glass was strangely in advance of its time; it is still being produced today.

Holland

The Dutch architect H. P. Berlage had been one of the pioneers of a truly Functionalist art of building, and already before the First World War, progressive Dutch architects were intimately familiar with the new style. After the war Functionalism was widely accepted also in the applied arts. The Royal Dutch Glass Works at Leerdam, near Rotterdam (founded in 1765), is the only factory to produce tableware and decorative glass in Holland, and its production was soon brought into line with the new development of style. Just before the First World War, P. M. Cochius became its director, and he began at once to take an active interest in modernizing the production. In 1915 he commissioned the progressive architect K. P. C. de Bazel to design tableware for Leerdam. Of extreme Functionalist severity were the services and vases designed from 1917 by Cornelis de Lorm (1875–1942), while the potter C. J. Lanooy (1881–1948) produced some robust models with coloured decorations. Berlage himself had designed table-glass for the French factories of Baccarat and Pantin as early as 1900. In 1923 he provided Leerdam with designs for tableware, his models being sturdy and simple and intended for execution in yellow glass.

The earliest pieces of a more ambitious character to be made at Leerdam were the 'jaarbeckers' or memorial glasses for each year, first produced in 1918, and made in heavy crystal, colourless or lightly tinted and with engraved or gilt inscriptions. The real pioneer in Dutch art glass seems to have been Chris Lebeau (1878–1945), a general designer who worked for Leerdam in 1922 and 1923. One group of his glasses seems to hark back to the *Art Nouveau*; they are exaggeratedly elongated in shape and have iridescent surfaces. Others are simpler, though without the mathematical formal clarity of Functionalism, and with mottled surfaces (Plate 49B). Lebeau was perhaps also responsible for the crackled and cased glass mentioned in contemporary writings. A full investigation of Lebeau's contribution to modern art glass is yet to come; when it does, it is sure to reveal some interesting things.

It was during Lebeau's time at Leerdam that the so-called 'Unica studio' was first established, and at his departure in 1923, Andries D. Copier (b. 1901) became its leader, a position which he has occupied until quite recently. He first became attached to the factory in 1914 as a designer of simple tableware. In the early Unica pieces he never ventured into audacious technical experiments or complicated methods of decoration. Preferring a fairly thin, transparent metal, perhaps tinted one colour, he produced a series of sober and graceful vases, some of them with moulded ribs and curved outlines. Others of his works show the impact of Functionalism. Flower vases in the shape of a perfect sphere were made by innumerable glass factories in many countries during the 'thirties, but Copier's model from 1928 must be one of the earliest examples.

U.S.A.

In 1933 the Steuben factory in the state of New York began the production of art glass in a modern style. The factory was founded in 1903 by a Stourbridge glassmaker with the express purpose of making decorative glass. In 1918 it had been absorbed as its art division into the vast concern of the Corning Glass Works. Up to 1933 the products had tended to be over-decorated and lacked consistent style, but the factory's technical resources were very great. In 1932 the production manager Robert J. Leavy had created a new transparent crystal, heavy and fat, softly toned and with a distinctly individual character. This became the basis for the new art production. The moving spirit in its conception was Arthur Amory Houghton, jun., the great-grandson of the founder of the works at Corning. He started from the principle that production and design should be separated in different departments, to prevent the products from becoming mere exercises in craftsmanship. The young architect John Monteith Gates became the factory's chief designer, with the sculptor Sidney Waugh at his side. During the first few years of their collaboration, the production was mainly experimental, but some fine engraved pieces were made. Waugh's 'Gazelle Vase' from 1935 harks back to Hald's style of engraving at Orrefors, and is a fine example of early Steuben art glass. 1936 saw the establishment of a Design Department with branches both in New York and at Corning, and with George Thompson as leader. While Gates and Waugh concentrated on designs for engraved decorations, Thompson devoted himself to the designing of forms; at times independent artists were asked to provide designs for engraving (Plate 82B). The full impact of the organization is, however, best seen in the post-war products of Steuben.

Germany

Between 1925 and 1930 the glass department of the Württembergische Metallwarenfabrik near Geislingen produced a series of fine individual pieces, made of fairly heavy material with inlaid colours and air-bubbles in firmly organized patterns (Plates 48, 49A). The genre was called 'Ikora', and it is said to have been the result of inspired teamwork among the factory's technicians under the leadership of the manager, Hugo Debach. The affinity with the Graal glass from Orrefors is obvious, but the Ikora products have a distinctive individuality, and it is to be regretted that their production was so shortlived.

ITALIAN RENAISSANCE

We have already seen how the old Venetian colour-techniques were revived about 1830, and how they became the major inspiring force when a new art of colour-glass was developed in France. In 1860 Antonio Salviati (1816–1900) had begun a large scale commercial production of glass in the traditional Venetian styles. Most of his models were over-elaborate in form and gaudy in colour, and the majority of the glass-makers in Murano followed him in making pastiches of seventeenth- and eighteenth-century Venetian glass mainly for sale to foreign tourists. A small production of glass in a simple and restrained style was, however, going on in Murano at the same time. A few of Salviati's models of this period were made of clear glass and formed into plain shapes with a few, well-placed glassblowers' ornaments as decoration; others were straight-forward exercises in the classic colour-techniques of Murano (Plate 50B). Andrea Rioda (d. 1921) and the firm of Artisti Barovier also favoured restraint and simplicity in their productions. After the First World War this dignified traditionalism received stimulating impulses from Functionalist ideas, and a truly modern style in glass was firmly established in Murano. Its creators were Paolo Venini (1895–1959) and Ercole Barovier (b. 1889).

P. Venini

Paolo Venini was born near Milan of a family which had old connections with the glass industry. He was himself destined for the law, but in 1921 he entered into partnership with a young Venetian business man, Giacomo Cappellin (b. 1887), to begin in Murano a production of glass in a simple style. For the customers of his shop in Milan, Cappellin had been giving commissions to Andrea Rioda for the making of imitations of the simple, utilitarian vessels in transparent glass, made in Venice during the early sixteenth century, and now chiefly known from the paintings of the Venetian masters of the period. Cappellin got the idea of taking over Rioda's furnace, and starting a production of simple, traditional glass with Rioda as technical director, and in November 1921 the firm of 'Vetri Soffiati Muranesi Cappellin-Venini & C.' began its activities, but without Rioda, who had just died. The Muranese designer Vittorio Zecchin (1878–1947), who had some knowledge of modern decorative work as well as of the production of glass, joined the firm as artistic director. Some of the early Cappellin-Venini models were copied from the ewers, urns and vases in old Venetian pictures, while others were free variations in their style; they were produced in transparent glass, either colourless or tinted an azure blue, a light green or a pale amethyst colour (Plate 51B). A selection of this glass was shown at the Paris Exhibition in 1925, and Venini and his associates were hailed as interesting young experimentalists. In the same year Venini parted company with Cappellin, and established his own factory, 'Venini & C.', in Murano.

There was at that time a tremendous will to modernism in progressive circles in Milan. Gio Ponti designed furniture and decorations in an angular and unornamented style which was superficially 'Functionalistic' and closely related to the fashionable modernism in Paris and Vienna. A main centre for the style in Milan was the firm of Fontana d'Arte (S.A. Luigi Fontana & C.) with Pietro Chiesa as artistic director; he designed furniture, light-fittings and all kinds of expensive decorative work in plate glass and mosaic, which were eagerly bought by a rich and fashion-conscious *clientèle*. To encourage modern design, an exhibition of decorative art, intended to be a bi-annual event, was organized in 1923 in Monza just outside Milan; in 1933 it was launched in Milan itself as a 'Triennale'. Together with the periodical *Domus*, started by Gio Ponti in 1928, the Milan Triennale became the main means of making Italian style in the applied arts known abroad. Venini worked in close contact with the Milan *milieu*, and his activities must be seen against this background.

After 1925, Venini discarded the purism of the early period, and began to exploit effects of colour and texture. He revived old Venetian colour-techniques, such as *millefiori* (or *murrine*, as the Romans said and as it is called in modern Murano) and *latticino*, and he invented new ones. *Vetro pulegoso* (1928) is an opaque, loose-textured substance with many small, close air-bubbles (Plate 52). *Vetro corroso* (1933) is treated with chemicals to give a corroded surface (Plate 51A) and *vetro sommerso* (1934) is bubbly glass, encased in some transparent material (Plate 50A). His new glass variations were used for vessels of extremely simple forms, distantly related to classical urns, or truly Functionalist in their extreme plainness. A small vase of irregular shape, designed for the Milan Triennale in 1933 (Plate 51A), marks perhaps his first departure from absolute sobriety of form, and after that time, graceful caprice took an increasingly important place in his repertoire. His basic programme remained, however, the same: simplicity of form, infinite variety of colour and texture.

At times Venini called in professional artists to design for him. The most spectacular results of his collaboration with the sculptor Napoleone Martinuzzi (from 1928 onwards) were some large-scale figures very amusingly constructed over a metal framework on the principle of the old Venetian chandeliers. A plant in *vetro pulegoso* was made in 1928 (Plate 52), and a dancing figure of Anna Pavlova at the Hotel Excelsior on the Lido in 1929. The architect Tommaso Buzzi assisted Venini to prepare his collection for the Triennale in 1933, where some interesting new colour-combinations were shown. Between 1934 and 1940 the Swedish potter Tyra Lundgren produced some charming designs for fishes and leaves (Plate 65B), some of which are still in production. Venini was, however, always to a large extent his own designer, and when he did employ outsiders he supervised the production so closely himself, that every product which left the factory was an unmistakable Venini model, with the technical perfection, precision of form and expressiveness of colour which have become hallmarks of his work. At the outbreak of the Second World War, Venini had two factories with altogether twelve masters, one of whom, Arturo Biasiutto, or 'Boboli', was said to be the cleverest glassblower in Murano.

Venini's followers

Venini's artistic and commercial success inspired other Murano glass-makers to embrace a more modern style.

In 1931, the firm of Salviati produced some vases of the chastest of forms, and during the years that followed Dino Martens designed for the firm some freely blown models in what can be described as a simplified traditional style. In 1934 the factory made opaque-white glass in abstract modernistic shapes. The firm Ferro Toso also worked on modern lines in blown glass. Zecchin designed table-glass with a distinct flavour of Joseph Hoffmann's Viennese modernism (see p. 62) for the firms of Arte Vetraria Muranese (AVEM) and Fratelli Toso. The Bohemian engraver F. Pelzel has since 1925 been attached to the glass-decorating firm of SALIR, while Guido Balsamo Stella (1882–1941), who did engraved glass in Venice in the early 'twenties (Plate 53B), designed for SALIR during the early part of the following decade. Through his Swedish-born wife he had a first-hand knowledge of the Swedish genre of engraving, and his style in the 'thirties was obviously derived from Orrefors, though it had neither the grandeur of Gate's works, nor the crispness of Hald's.

In 1934 Flavio Poli (b. 1900) was appointed art manager of the Murano firm of Seguso Vetri d'Arte. He had worked in other fields, among them ceramics, before he concentrated on glass. He designed rich, semi-sculptural forms with colour-inlay and air-bubbles inside the walls of the vessels (Plate 54); often metallic effects were added. Poli's style of the 'thirties is sometimes reminiscent of Marinot's.

Ercole Barovier

The only glassmaker in Murano between the wars who can be compared to Venini for artistic talent and independence of taste is Ercole Barovier, at present administrative and artistic director of the firm of Barovier & Toso. He comes from an old Murano glassmaking family which can be traced back to the fifteenth century, and his father, Benvenuto Barovier, had been head of the progressive firm of Artisti Barovier (see p. 54). During the 'twenties Barovier began to search for new effects of texture and colour, and he invented some very interesting varieties. In 1927 he created his *primavera* glass, light and graceful in substance and with an attractive mottled surface (Plate 53A); in 1940 came his transparent *rugiada* glass with an effect like fine dew on the surface (Plate 55B), *vetro gemmato* (1936–8) with an uneven surface, reminiscent of the texture of natural stone (Plate 55A), glass with inlaid gold reliefs and many other new genres. Ercole Barovier's shapes from this time are usually simple, but without the determined austerity and precision of the Venini products of the same period. Barovier's glass is always gently fluid, and there is something natural and unforced about his work which sets it in a class apart. Genuine sculptural qualities can be traced in many of his models.

Spain

The only noteworthy Spanish glass artist of the period was José Maria Gol, of Barcelona. He made some fanciful vessels in imaginative furnace work, following the tradition of old Spanish glass, and also produced spirited flower patterns or purely abstract designs in enamel-painting, using brilliant colours, applied to the glass with a broad and 'impressionistic' brush (Plate 58B).

THE STRONGHOLDS OF TRADITION

Britain

Since the invention in London some three hundred years ago of the heavy, transparent and sonorous lead crystal, this has been the standard metal of all British factories, and its qualities have almost exclusively decided the form and decoration of their products. During the eighteenth century a style of cutting was evolved which brought out in a new way the wonderful refractory qualities of lead glass; the genre became widespread and between *c.* 1730 and 1830 new patterns were being developed all the time. The fashion for cut glass continued into the succeeding age, but with the rise in output and with the extended use of machinery, the style became increasingly stereotyped. By the time of the great Exhibition in 1851, glass factories all over Britain were turning out vast masses of big unwieldy vases, bowls and table-glass, heavily decorated with criss-cross patterns cut deeply into the glass and polished to a hard, glittering brilliance. With small alterations this kind of glass remained the standard product in Britain far into the twentieth century. For the last hundred years or more, the Midland town of Stourbridge has been the centre of the production of cut crystal, and factories in other parts of Britain have followed suit. In spite of its lack of artistic vigour, the English cut-glass style remained very popular, and it was taken up by makers of many nations. Until quite recently, the English type of heavy cut crystal represented the ideal of fine and precious glass to the broad public in most western and some eastern countries.

The most important modernization in the production of British lead crystal in the twentieth century was a technical one. In 1915 a Department for Glass Technology was established at the University of Sheffield under the inspiring leadership of Professor W. E. S. Turner; the Society of Glass Technology was founded in 1916. Thanks to the activities of these bodies, scientific methods have been grafted on to the old empirical tradition, and the quality of the crystal has been greatly improved. Technical progress has, however, not been accompanied by a corresponding renewal of style; the even greater technical perfection of the traditional material has rather made it more of a 'fetish' to its producers than before. In 1935 the establishment of an art section of the Society of Glass Technology was discussed, but the idea seemed fruitless. The whole industry with its staff and equipment was so firmly geared to the production of cut crystal, that it was impossible to break away from the old accepted style. 'English glass, except in one or two famous cases, is clumsy and ornate in design, and expensive,' wrote an angry critic in 1938. 'The uses of table-glass are much what they were a hundred years ago or more.' The 'one or two famous cases' were, we must assume, the fine simple glass made at the firm of Whitefriars in London, and the handsome table-services and decorative glass made at the Stourbridge factory of Stevens & Williams to the designs of Keith Murray.

The production of glass with furnace-worked decoration in a tasteful *fin de siècle* style, which had begun at the factory of Whitefriars about 1880 (see p. 33) was continued until well after the First World War. A new era in the factory's history began when James Hogan (1883–1948) became director. Hogan had been attached to Whitefriars from the age of fifteen, mainly in the department for stained glass, and he had supplemented his practical experience with a formal art education at the Central School of Art in London. Apart from making designs for stained-glass windows, James Hogan created a new style for the factory's section for blown glass, which soon began to gain its makers laurels in exhibitions at home and abroad. A heavily fluid transparent lead metal was formed into plain, well-proportioned vessels, most of which had a useful purpose; sometimes simple furnace-worked decorations were added, while cut or engraved ornaments were rare. The style, which was reminiscent of English glass from the early eighteenth century, was truly functional, but without the hard angularity or other external trimmings of much Functionalist design of the 'thirties. It was quickly absorbed by the factory's staff, and fine designs in the characteristic idiom were produced by Barnaby Powell (1891–1939) (Plate 59B), the last representative of the Powell dynasty, and by Hogan's co-director, William J. Wilson. Sometimes the factory's best glassblower, Tom Hill, who has worked for the firm since 1929, collaborated in the creation of new models.

It was after having seen the Exhibition in Paris in 1925 that the young architect Keith Murray (b. New Zealand 1893) began to ask himself why English glass in the conventional style was so unsatisfactory to him; the

Swedish Exhibition in London in 1931 further increased his interest in a modern style of glass. He began to analyse old English glass, which had long been a hobby of his, to find out why it was so good, and he came to the conclusion that it was satisfying if left plain; if it were cut, it was good if cut into a 'well-organized decoration', flat cutting being particularly advantageous, as it did not disturb the clarity of the glass. Early in 1932 he began to make designs for table-glass 'with ultimate purpose', and Whitefriars produced a few experimental pieces for him, but the designs were not suitable for the processes in use at their works. The idea of the artist designing for industry was, however, beginning to be accepted in England. One of the champions of modern design in England, the furniture-maker Gordon Russell, had designed both ornamental ware and table-glass, which had been produced in small quantities by Whitefriars as well as by the firm of Stevens & Williams at Brierley Hill, near Stourbridge. In 1932 it was arranged that Murray should work as a designer of glass for Stevens & Williams for three months of the year.

Murray's first designs had been made before he had any real knowledge of glass and how it was made, and they needed important adjustments before they could be put into production. But when he began to pay prolonged visits to the works in order to familiarize himself with the material and the methods of working it, he was delighted to find a willing response to his ideas among the workmen themselves, who seemed pleased to apply their skill to the making of fresh products. After 'a period of alterations and editings, in which I had to adapt myself to the material and its processes, and in which the factory had to adapt itself to my conception of form,' glass made to Murray's designs began to flow from the factory.

Murray's production during the seven years he worked with glass includes both table-services and more ambitious pieces. Generally speaking, he was more interested in form than in decoration. His table-services were simple and sane and mostly unornamented. For bigger pieces he sometimes favoured simple, freeblown forms; some of them were produced in green glass, and varied with moulded surface decorations, which hark back to the gentle style of Copier at Leerdam and Bang's work at Holmegaard. A few models are expressly of their time, showing the fashionable colour-contrast of black against transparent glass (Plate 57B). When he tried his hand at designs for engraving, the patterns were simple, some with a touch of angular modernism, but most of them very graceful and charming, and distributed evenly over the whole surface of the vessels (Plate 57A). Designs with the cactus (a favourite plant in the 'thirties) as motif form a separate group, with the patterns slashed deeply, almost aggressively, into the surface (Plate 57B). Murray's most important glasses are, however, the large vases and dishes of heavy metal, decorated with flat cutting, reminiscent of early Georgian work (Plate 56). Here his architectural feeling has found powerful expression, and the *décor* underlines the properties of the material in an authoritative way.

During the 'thirties Murray designed a few pieces of silver for the firm of Mappin & Webb in London, as well as a number of pottery models for Wedgwood's. During the late 'thirties he became architect to Wedgwood's new factory in Stoke-on-Trent; he became less and less able to give time to industrial design, and at the outbreak of war in 1939 he gave it up altogether.

Other efforts at exploiting the talents of contemporary artists in the production of glass were made in preparation for the exhibition of 'British Art in Industry' which was organized by the Royal Society of Arts in Burlington House in the spring of 1935. Apart from some fine glass from Whitefriars and a large section of Brierley Crystal made to Keith Murray's designs, there was glass designed by Paul Nash and Graham Sutherland, Dame Laura Knight and Eric Ravilious for the firm of Stuart & Sons in Stourbridge. But the reviewer, M. L. Anderson, writing in *Design for To-day*, the main periodical for modern design at the time, was not enthusiastic. Many of the artist-designers, he said, had obviously a very short experience of the material of glass, and had had no time for experimentation, and their works showed the faults inevitable in products that were the fruits of too short a partnership between artist-designer and manufacturer. Speaking generally about the glass section he noted with satisfaction that an increased attention was being paid to pure shape at the cost of ornamentation, while he reflected on the limited use of colour, which was such an important feature in contemporary glass on the Continent, the only coloured glass in Burlington House being some pieces in amber, designed by James Hogan for the firm of Whitefriars. The exhibition did much to explain the importance of good design in industrial goods to the British public, but as far as glass was concerned the effects were not lasting. During the later 'thirties, the only professional glass designer in Britain, apart from Keith Murray, was Clyne Farquharson, who did some simple and dignified vases with cut and engraved patterns for the firm of John Walsh Walsh in Stourbridge (Plate 59A), and later for Stevens & Williams.

Strangely outside the main stream of British glassmaking between the two World Wars was the so-called 'Monart' glass, which was produced from 1923 onwards by the Scottish firm of John Moncrieff in Perth. In 1922 Salvador Ysart (1877–1955), a glassmaker from Barcelona, joined the firm, where he produced a series of decorative pieces, oxidized with coloured marble-like effects in the Venetian-Mediterranean tradition. Many of the designs were suggested by Mrs. Moncrieff. The best examples from the early period (Plate 58A) are very fine indeed. The production has continued up to the present day, now with Salvador Ysart's sons as makers.

The German-speaking countries.

At about the same time as Ravenscroft's invention of lead glass took place in England, a similarly heavy, transparent glass was created in the Bohemian-Silesian area where it provided the stimulus for a spectacular development in the arts of cutting and engraving. Glass with cut facets and engraved figures was soon made in many parts of the German-speaking areas, and during the eighteenth century it was exported to all the corners of the earth. The nineteenth century saw the adoption by the Bohemian factories of the English style of heavy cutting, which was developed to an unsurpassed virtuosity. The style has survived until our own day in Bohemia in the extensive range of export wares, which is a chief part of the production. And Bohemia still provides the finest engravers and cutters to countries where these crafts have a less firm tradition.

During the first decade of the twentieth century, a fresh stylistic impulse came from Vienna to the glass factories in Bohemia (which in 1918 became the independent state of Czechoslovakia). The chief inventor of the modern Viennese style was the architect and designer Josef Hoffmann (b. 1870), founder-member in 1897 of the union of radical Viennese artists called the Wiener Sezession, and in 1903 of the business organization of the Wiener Werkstätte, which provided workshops for the practical production of the works of progressive designers. Hoffmann was an early pioneer of a Functionalist style in decoration: even before 1900 he had advocated basic geometric figures like the square and the circle as particularly suitable for ornaments. As early as 1900 he occupied himself with glass. Through his activities as teacher at the Wiener Kunstgewerbeschule, (the Viennese School for Applied Arts), he became a powerful influence. Heavy angular forms soon became favoured in the Bohemian glass factories, and in decoration his geometric style was grafted on to the graceful neoclassicism traditional in Vienna; the result was a pretty figure style with dressed or undressed females in coquettish poses, simplified and stylized in form and perhaps placed within a framework of straight lines; purely geometric ornament was also used. This mildly modernistic decorative style became the standard idiom of the decorators in many materials who worked for Wiener Werkstätte; it was applied to glass by several artists, the most important among them being Michael Powolny (b. 1871), teacher in glass decoration at the Kunstgewerbeschule des Österreichischen Museums (the School for Applied Art of the Austrian Museum). The style was transmitted to the Bohemian glass industry by way of the schools for glassmaking and decoration in Haida and Steinschönau, while at the 'Fachschule' in Zwiesel, in Bavaria, it was given a personal and very graceful interpretation by Bruno Mauder, head of the school from 1910. At the Prager Kunstgewerbeschule (School for Applied Arts), the Viennese style had to compete with the grand classical style in engraving, which was traditional for the more ambitious works, and which was practised with particular mastery by Josef Drahoňovsky (b. 1877), an engraver on glass and precious stones and, from 1908, professor at the school in Prague.

'Wiener Stil' became widely popular in many European countries, and Edward Hald and Balsamo Stella in their designs for engraving, as well as Vittorio Zecchin in his glass shapes, all owe a debt to Vienna.

Through the activities of the firm of J. & L. Lobmeyr, Viennese taste and Bohemian craftsmanship were combined in the most fruitful way.

Since 1823 three generations of Lobmeyrs had worked as dealers in and refiners of glass in Vienna. The firm had always kept up a very high standard of taste and elegance; a dignified classical style had been consistently favoured for engraved decorations. The connection with the Wiener Kunstgewerbeschule had always been close, and both Josef Hoffmann and Michael Powolny designed for Lobmeyr. In 1918 Ludwig Lobmeyr's nephew Stephan Rath (b. 1876) founded a branch establishment in Steinschönau under the name of 'J. &. L. Lobmeyrs Neffe Stephan Rath', where glass was made to Rath's specification and decorated to the designs of artists by the finest engravers of the district. From 1920 to 1937 Rath's daughter, Marianne Rath (b. 1904) worked as designer for the firm. A fine, eight-lobed fruit dish, reminiscent of seventeenth-century silver in its form, is one of her earlier creations (Plate 60A), and she also suggested designs for pieces to be worked freely at the furnace. For the Paris Exhibition in 1925 Jaroslav Horejc (b. 1886), one of Drahoňovsky's pupils, did four vases with engraved decoration (Plate 61) in a magnificent classical style with figures in very high relief (*Hochschnitt*). Glass in a similar, but more dramatic style was designed about 1925 by Ena Rottenberg, like Horejc of Hungarian origin; she also designed furnace-worked shapes with engraved decoration closely wedded to the form of the glass (Plate 60B). Lotte Fink took up the grand classical style in some of her designs for engraving, and she also did some enamelled glass.

The new Lobmeyr glass was enthusiastically received in Paris in 1925, and the firm continued the production of glass in the same style until 1945, when their contact with the Bohemian glass industry was severed. It still carries on its production of glass, now provided from Austrian factories, with fine engraved decoration.

An engraver of more than equal stature to the Stephan Rath group was Wilhelm v. Eiff (1890–1943). He was the son of a craftsman at the Göppingen branch of the Württembergische Metallwarenfabrik, and he learned the technique of engraving on both metal and glass at a very early age, while the local drawing school gave him his first formal art education. He then spent some years wandering over Europe, working wherever he could find congenial employment; he spent some time in Lalique's jeweller's studio, and for another period he worked with the famous glass engraver Charles Michel in Paris. In 1913 he paid a short visit to the Art School in Stuttgart, where he was inspired by the teaching of the famous Munich designer, Bernhard Pankok. The same year saw his earliest contact with Stephan Rath, with whom he worked for a time in 1921. In 1922 v. Eiff became professor in cutting and engraving on glass and precious stones at the school in Stuttgart.

v. Eiff was an idealistic lover of all the arts: he was musical and apart from his real *métier* of cutting and engraving, he practised both painting and the graphic arts. Through his sovereign mastery as a craftsman of all branches and grades of cutting and engraving on glass, he was able to use his tools in free artistic expression, and being himself both the designer and the executor of his works, he could give them a deeply individual character, which sets them in a class apart. He engraved the fine details in a miniature portrait with incredible finesse, while the traditional technique of cutting were used in new and highly personal ways (Plates 62B, 63). His finest achievement is, however, his work in high relief (*Hochschnitt*) where the technique of engraving has lost its character of a miniature art and acquired the power and dignity of sculpture (Plate 62A). During the late 'thirties he invented a new tool for engraving, which could be wielded freely in the hand, and which made possible the execution of engraved windows on a monumental scale.

As professor in Stuttgart, v. Eiff exercised a great influence on his pupils, who came to learn from him in ever-increasing numbers. He seems to have been able to fire them with an enthusiasm, not only for the art of cutting and engraving, but for the material of glass itself. Today pupils of his are working all over the world, from Scotland to Japan, doing original and creative work in styles and techniques which differ widely from each other's as well as from v. Eiff's own work.

3

NEO-FUNCTIONALISM: 1945-1960

The Second World War was accompanied by no change of style as decisive as the arrival of Functionalism; we are still elaborating on the main ideas which were generally established in architecture and the applied arts round about 1915. That there should be an intimate connection between form, material and practical function is now taken for granted; simplicity of form and purity of outline are still purposely sought after, and textural effects are stressed at the cost of external ornament. But the classical norms of proportion and rhythm, which were so closely integrated into Functional aesthetics in the early stages, are now displaced by new conceptions of form and their interrelationships; the inspiration seems to derive partly from oriental and primitive art, partly from aeroplane and rocket construction. The heavy angularity of early Functionalism has been discarded, and lightness of form is being increasingly preferred, with an emphasis on slimness which sometimes finds expression in exaggeratedly elongated shapes. The serious intellectualism of the early 'twenties is likewise a past stage, and a new mood of gentle lyricism is becoming increasingly prevalent; elegance of line is sought for its own sake, and colours have become deep and subtly shaded, and often possess more than a touch of emotionalism. Designers in Italy, Finland and Sweden have been chiefly instrumental in creating this post-war phase of Functionalism, and glass has been an important medium of expression in the process.

Italy

Venini retained his leading position among the glassmakers in Murano. His programme remained the same – simplicity of form, infinite variety of colour and texture – and he continued to pursue it with unfailing

C. *Vase with coloured stripes, by Venini,* 1959
Ht. 12 *ins. Mr and Mrs A. Gumb, London*
(*See page* 67)

enthusiasm, inventiveness and boldness of taste (Colour plate C), until the time of his death in 1959. Though he still on occasion called in professional designers to assist him, he was always the chief creative element in the factory. Among his new techniques were *vetro tessuto*, of which experimental pieces were made in 1940 to the design of Carlo Scarpa, with threads of glass in contrasting colours embedded in the glass (Plate 65A), and *vetro pezzato* with a patchwork effect of squares in different colours (Plate 64A), which first appeared at the Triennale in Milan in 1951. Sometimes the colours of Venini's post-war glass are toned up to a brightness which only his unfailing taste saves from being glaring. A very popular model, dating from 1946, is the so-called 'folded handkerchief', where a square of glass with patterns in *latticino* or with a casing of one bright colour over an opaque-white base has been loosely 'folded' into the shape of a vase (Plate 64B). The form has been copied and debased by numerous other makers, but the best Venini examples are exquisite things.

Ercole Barovier has increasingly established himself as an artist of equal stature to Venini. Eleven masters at two wood-fired furnaces, together with a team of chemist-engineers, realize his ideas. Barovier prefers soft, subdued tones of moss-green, brown and even black, and he experiments freely with textural effects. *Vetro barbarico* is opaque with a rough surface, *vetro ramarro* or 'lizard glass' is green and mottled, *vetro damasco* has mosaic effects of coloured glass and a dusting of gold (Plate 67A), while *vetro parabolico* (Plate 67B) is a personal version of patchwork glass. The shapes are freely and simply formed; at times they approach pure sculpture. His son Angelo (b. 1927) has joined him as designer to Barovier & Toso. He is a painter in his own right, and many of his models reveal the independent artist.

At the firm of Seguso Vetri d'Arte, Flavio Poli is still head designer, and his style has developed towards ever greater clarity and precision since the war. He works in a heavier material than that which is normal in Murano, and the forms are more firmly defined, without that air of improvisation which otherwise is such a characteristic feature of Venetian glass (Plate 66B). His attachment to the Venetian tradition reveals itself most clearly in his subtle use of colour, which he is apt to apply sparingly on otherwise transparent vessels to accentuate special points of build and construction (Plate 66A).

Several other firms in Murano have done imaginative things in a modern idiom. The Milan Triennale has been an important stimulus to this kind of work, but few makers keep up the steady flow of interesting models of Venini, the Baroviers and Flavio Poli.

During the last few years Luciano Gaspari has designed smooth, plain models of heavy glass for Salviati's factory. Dino Martens, a painter, who designed for Salviati before the war, has been resident designer for the firm of Aureliano Toso during later years. Especially striking among his imaginative models are his patchwork vessels, where each 'patch' has a pattern of its own, frequently in *latticino*. Alberto Toso has produced some robust models with spirals in bold colours, while Archimede Seguso favours a dignified and noble traditionalism in his designs for his own factory. In his models for Arte Vetraria Muranese (AVEM) Giulio Radi (d. 1952) made extensive use of metallic effects applied like dust to the surface of his vessels. These are of highly imaginative shapes and made of a heavy, non-transparent material in deep, glowing colours. His glass is sometimes bizarre, but the best pieces have an impressive richness and maturity.

For the decorating firm of SALIR, engraved patterns have been designed by Romualdo Scarpa, Serena Dal Maschio, R. Licata and Tono Zancanaro, while Vinicio Vianello has created patterns of *cento lenti* or 'a hundred lenses', that is polished ovals or circles cut into a sandblasted ground. Vianello has also designed some strange irregular shapes in featherweight transparent glass for the firm of SALIR. In 1957 he started his own factory for useful glass.

For his own factory Gino Cenedese has designed some elaborate models, some of them in the form of naturalistic sculpture, others of abstract shapes which at times approach the form of vessels. He favours opaque glass with heavily treated surfaces – his glass is really conceived as a kind of stone. A typical Cenedese genre is glass with spirited designs in enamels embedded into heavy blocks of transparent glass. Recently Antonio da Ros has designed for Cenedese's factory some asymmetrical, coloured vases with heavy casings of transparent glass. In 1950 Alfredo Barbini, who used to work in Cenedese's factory, began working independently in a related style.

In 1950 'Il Centro Studio Pittori nell'arte del Vetro' was established, to bring the talents of artists to the glass furnaces of Murano. Designs have been submitted to the factories by a number of Italian artists and by some of the most famous names of the world today, among them Picasso, Kokoschka, Chagall, Alexander Calder and Le Corbusier. Some spirited results have been obtained, but the contacts have not been lasting.

To complete the picture of the extremely rich and varied world of glass in Italy, some decorators of glass should be mentioned. Since 1945 the Austrian-born artist Edwin Burger has worked independently in Milan. He cuts and engraves glass into sculptured forms of more or less naturalistic shapes, and he decorates glass vessels in these and other techniques. A pupil of Pietro Chiesa, Ranci Ortigosa, is now head designer to the Milan firm of Fontana d'Arte, while the firm of Stil Novo in Montelupo, near Florence, makes blanks from the glass factories into mosaic, lighting equipment and decorative vessels.

Finland

The founder of an original art of glass in Finland was Gunnel Nyman (1909–48), one of the most remarkable personalities in modern glass history. She trained at the Design School at Helsinki, and began as a designer of furniture, but after the death of Henry Ericsson, the head designer at Riihimäki, she began to design table-glass for the factory. Soon afterwards she won a competition for glass designs arranged by the Karhula-Iittala factory, and from that time onwards she dedicated her time increasingly to glass. Her earliest designs, which were shown at the Exhibition in Paris in 1937, were very fine, but not of striking originality. It was during a burst of creativeness between 1945 and 1947 that her most personal work in glass was done. By that time she had more or less a free hand; her models were executed at Riihimäki, Nuutajärvi or Iittala, whichever factory was most suitable for their realization, and ideas flowed freely from her hand. Her style varied from graceful lyricism to the strictest intellectual severity.

Gunnel Nyman worked in transparent glass, occasionally with touches of milky white. She had an intense feeling for the soft pliability of the material, as shown in her many 'folded' models (Plate 69A), while the effects of inlaid colours and bubbles were exploited in a series of graceful little vases. The technique of cutting was used in new and original ways. By dividing the surface of her vessel into irregularly intersecting planes, she devised fascinating possibilities of refraction, while the smooth brilliance of the glass was retained in the large undisturbed surfaces in between (Plate 69B). Whatever technique she employed, she gave to all her designs a subtle touch of true poetry.

The line struck out by Gunnel Nyman was pursued and further developed by a group of other Finnish designers after her untimely death at the age of forty. At the Milan Triennale in 1951, the Finns made a sensational showing and established themselves as among the world's leading makers of art glass. The dominating figure was Tapio Wirkkala

(b. 1915), from 1947 designer for Karhula-Iittala. Some of his models are cut in asymmetrical curves (Plate 70B), others are freely formed into the gentlest and lightest of shapes, with simple engraved lines to emphasize the form (Plate 71A); figure-engraving of an intensely emotional character is employed on massive, roughly hewn forms (Plate 68A). Wirkkala works in many materials; some of his finest work has been done in wood. His creative period in glass seems to have stopped soon after the Triennale in 1954, but his Iittala models have become classics.

The real sensation in the Finnish section in Milan in 1954 was Timo Sarpaneva (b. 1926), who was attached to Iittala from 1950 onwards. Executed in solid, transparent glass with some touches of milky white, his models at the Triennale were really abstract sculpture (Plate 70A), even if some of them were alleged to be flower-vases, and they showed a powerful, original talent. Since then Sarpaneva, who is also an eminent textile designer, has created his own very personal, but somewhat less exclusive style in glass. His later glasses, most of which have a useful purpose, rely for their exquisite effect on purity of line and material alone. He favours a thin, lightweight material, in subtle shades of mauve, grey or blue; the shapes are as simple as possible, but possess a perfect precision of line which makes them stand out among all similar products.

From 1951 Kaj Franck (b. 1911) has been art director at the factory of Nuutajärvi (Notsjö), where he has designed some excellent table-glass, and also some simple, sober vases of great dignity and charm.

Sweden

Orrefors is still the centre of the flourishing Swedish art-glass production, and in the designers' studio at the factory, the traditions from the heroic days of the 'twenties and 'thirties are carried on by some of the artists of that period, as well as by representatives of a new generation.

Simon Gate died in 1945, but Edward Hald, as head of the factory's art department, has done some fine work since the war, both in engraving and colour techniques (Plate 72). Nils Landberg, (b. 1907) has been attached to Orrefors as designer since 1936. He does windows and light-fittings, but he is also responsible for some exquisite vessels in elegantly elongated shapes, sometimes reminiscent of the *Art Nouveau*, and with subtly shaded colours. Edvin Öhrström carries on his production of robust models, some of them in complicated Graal and Ariel techniques, which clearly show the sculptor's sensitive touch. To Sven Palmqvist (b. 1906, at Orrefors since 1936) falls the honour of the latest of the factory's technical inventions, the so-called 'Ravenna' glass, which is employed in vessels of

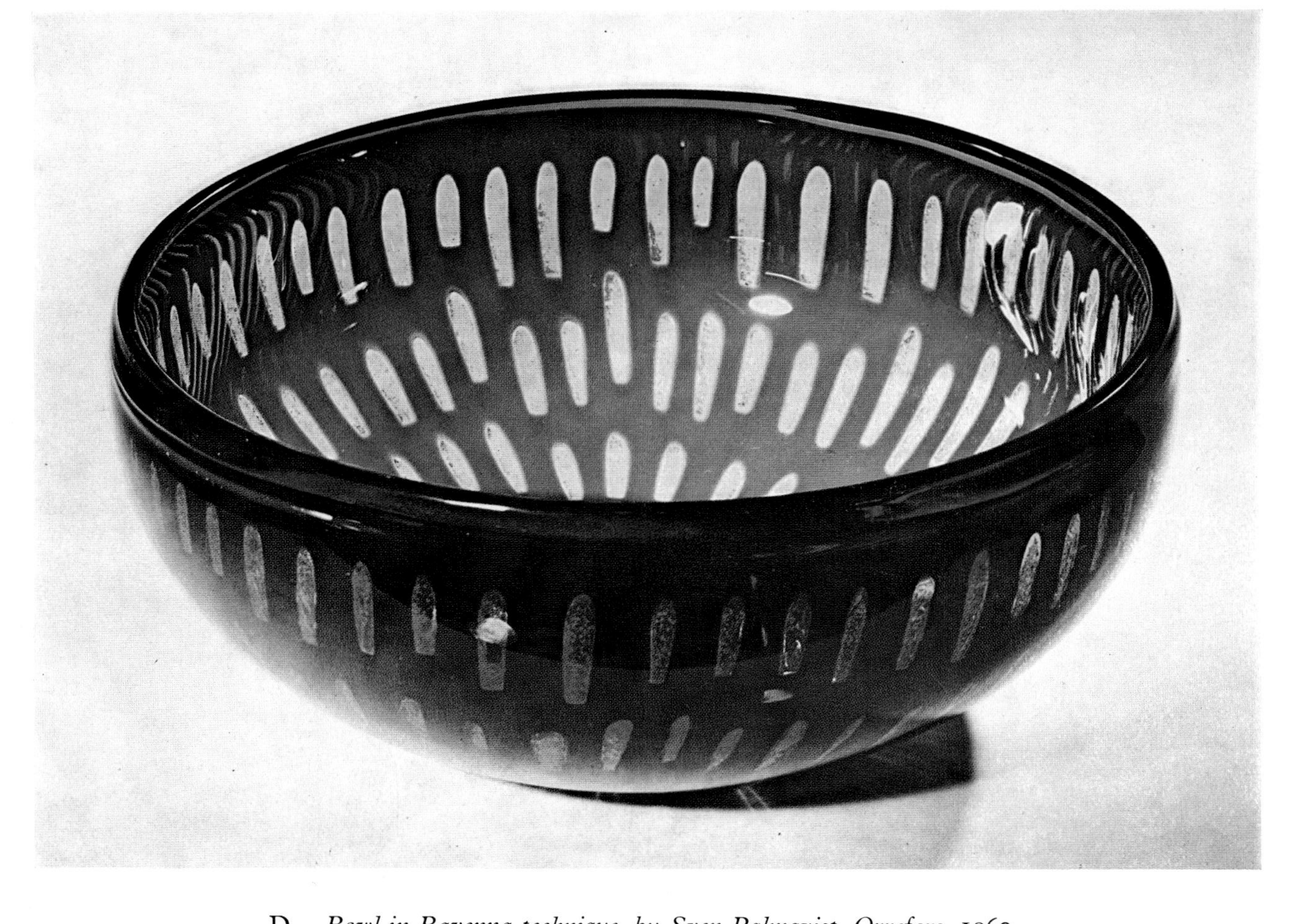

D. *Bowl in Ravenna technique, by Sven Palmqvist, Orrefors,* 1960
Ht. $4\frac{3}{4}$ *ins.*
(*See page* 71)

heavy glass, usually tinted to produce some transparent colour, into which are inlaid simple, non-figurative patterns in glowing, jewel-like hues (Colour plate D). The technique was finally worked out during the late 'forties, and it is one of the finest creations of the modern art of glass. In 1947 Ingeborg Lundin (b. 1921) joined the firm, and she has developed a style all her own. She is not interested in very complicated technical experiments. In lightly transparent glass she has made series of tall, conical figures, which become interesting mainly when put together in groups. When she employs engraving, it is a shallow scratching, which is more a textural treatment than an incision of patterns (Plate 73A). This genre of engraving has been successfully exploited by other artists at Orrefors, Öhrström among them (Plate 73B). Ingeborg Lundin also uses cutting to obtain an interesting texture. Her vessels are of the utmost simplicity, and rely on purity of line and perhaps one or two simple colours for their appeal. John Selbing (b. 1908), who has been attached to the factory since 1927, has designed some simple and tasteful models in transparent glass. In 1959, Gunnar Cyrén (b. 1931) became attached to Orrefors as designer.

Vicke Lindstrand, formerly at Orrefors, has been head designer at Kosta since 1950, and his output is impressive, in artistic variety as well as in sheer bulk. With wonderful inventiveness and the subtlest artistry he has employed all the techniques developed at Orrefors, cutting and engraving, Graal and Ariel, and combined and adjusted them to his own needs (Plate 74). At Kosta Lindstrand has developed the Orrefors idiom of the 'thirties to its utmost limit of sophisticated elegance. From 1953, Ernest Gordon (b. 1926), an Englishman and a graduate from the Royal College of Art in London, has been a designer of glass for Kosta, and in 1959 Mona Morales Schildt joined the firm.

Apart from Orrefors and Kosta, there are today more than a dozen factories in Sweden which produce glass under the direction of professional designers. Much of their talent goes into the making of good table-glass, where the general quality is very high. Most of these firms do on occasion make more ambitious models, mostly for serial production. Hugo Gehlin (d. 1953) at Gullaskruf did fine things in free furnace work (Plate 75A), and Arthur Percy made elegant engraved glass for the same firm (Plate 75B), while Bengt Orup at Johansfors, John-Orwar Lake and many others are doing excellent work in the well-established Swedish manner. Erik Höglund (b. 1932) has worked for Boda since 1953. His most characteristic models are thrown off, quickly and casually, in the simplest of techniques, blowing or moulding, and decorated with gay, even facetious motifs in shallow engraving. There is today a general tendency in Swedish glass away from technically complicated art glass towards plain and simple vessels, most of them with some useful purpose, basic in form and executed in transparent, perhaps tinted, material. Monica Bratt at Reijmyre and Nils Landberg at Orrefors have done some fine work in this manner. But its most important exponent is of course Strömbergshyttan, where the course struck out by its founder in the 'thirties is being pursued with unswerving consistency. Until a few years ago Gerda Strömberg (d. 1960) was the factory's chief designer, a fact which ensured continuity from Edvard Strömberg's time. Since 1953 Gunnar Nylund (b. 1904), famous as a pottery designer, has worked for Strömbergshyttan (Plate 77B), while Mrs. Asta Strömberg is responsible for many models in the factory's pre-war style.

Norway

After the war the factory of Hadeland greatly enlarged its output of art glass, and struck out a new line in design with an increased stress on colour-glass and furnace work at the cost of extrinsic decoration. Willy Johansson and Herman Bongard were engaged as designers in 1947. Willy Johansson (b. 1921) is the son of Wilhelm Johansson, a master glass-blower at the factory, who has himself done some original work; he is a graduate from the College of Art in Oslo. Apart from giving a new sobriety and elegance to the factory's range of table-glass, Johansson has created many interesting art-glass models, some charming vases with inlaid colours and varied textural effects, as well as bottles and vases made of ruby-red glass that changes to sea-green in the lower parts of the vessel. This genre gained him a *diplôme d'honneur* at the Milan Triennale in 1954. Herman Bongard (b. 1921) has designed regularly for the factory between 1947 and 1955. He works in pottery, silver and wood as well as in glass. Many of Bongard's models have broad, flattened forms, whose sides give a good background for inlaid coloured ornaments (Plate 79A). Arne Jon Jutrem (b. 1929) has worked for Hadeland since 1950. His vase of transparent glass with 'prickles' from 1951 is a spirited piece of work (Plate 78A). Today he favours simple, robust shapes, well suited for execution in bubbled green glass (Plate 78B); his recent vessels of transparent glass with spirals in colours are also interesting (Plate 79B). His designs for engraving and sandblasting have abstract patterns in a rough and sketchy technique. The young Severin Brörby is also working in colour techniques as well as in engraving, and he has shown great promise, especially in the latter genre. The architect Jonas Hidle is chief designer of lighting-equipment and occasionally designs vessels.

The factory Norsk Glassverk at Magnor near the Swedish border has produced table-glass and decorative vessels since 1950, with the all-round artist Arne Lindaas as first designer. Eystein Sandberg was head designer between 1951 and 1955, when the production was enlarged. He was succeeded by Axel Mörch. These three designers have done some good work in furnace-worked glass with inlaid colours.

Denmark

In 1942 Jacob Bang left Holmegaard, and Per Lütken became the factory's head designer in his stead. At first Lütken followed closely in Bang's footsteps, creating models with plain, severe shapes and with simple cut decoration. He became, however, increasingly fascinated by the fluidity of his material, and for a time during the middle 'fifties he designed a series of furnace-worked models whose shapes were almost exaggeratedly twisted and convoluted (Plate 94B). Lately he has settled down to a more restrained style of blown glass, which is not aggressively 'individual', and the difference between decorative and useful glass is not always distinct. Since 1955 Jacob Bang has designed glass for the factory of Kastrup. Until Bang joined it, this old firm was mainly occupied in producing bottles for the Danish breweries. Bang's Kastrup models are simple and sober like his Holmegaard glass, but softer and more gentle (Plate 94A). He is being assisted by Bent Severin and a team of young designers, Elisabeth Sass, Hans H. Henriksen and others, who all produce simple, blown models in a lightweight, sometimes tinted material. Since 1936 Åse Voss Schrader has run an engraver's shop in Copenhagen, where she has done some charming work. She was a pupil of v. Eiff's in Stuttgart, and she practises both wheel-engraving and diamond-point (Plate 68B). Bente Bonné is her pupil.

Germany

The same quest for simplicity, the return to the basic qualities of glass and glassblowing, which is noticeable in Finland, Sweden and Denmark, can also be seen in the glass factories in Western Germany.

Wilhelm Wagenfeld (b. 1900) works as designer at the Württembergische Metallwarenfabrik. Trained at the Bauhaus and the Kunstgewerbeschule in Stuttgart, he has inherited a sober sense of form and a profound feeling for the special properties of glass as an artist's material, and his simple, elegant glass forms bear witness to this. Wagenfeld also designs for the glass factory recently attached to the Rosenthal porcelain factory in Taunus and for the table-glass and lampshade factory Peill &

Putzler in the Rhineland. Wagenfeld's younger colleagues at the Württembergische Metallwarenfabrik, Erich Jachmann (b. 1925) and Sigrid Kupetz (b. 1926) cultivate an equally simple, austere style. At the Gralglashütte at Göppingen Th. Baumann (b. 1924) and Josef Stadler work in a similar formal idiom. Yet another representative of the simple and sober German style of today is Richard Süssmuth (b. 1900), who was trained at Dresden. He started his own factory in 1924 and his present establishment in Kassel was founded in 1946. Albin Schaedel (b. 1905) makes some slightly more elaborate models of great elegance at his factory at Arnstadt in Thuringia, while Emile Rimpler (b. 1911) produces decorated glass at his factory at Zwiesel in Bavaria.

The German tradition of decorated glass is best represented by a group of v. Eiff's pupils. Konrad Habermeier (b. 1907), his assistant, designs for Gralglashütte and is director of the glass-division of the Staatliche höhere Fachschule für das Edelmetallgewerbe (National High School for Metal Work) in Schwäbisch Gmünd. He designs the simplest of shapes (Plate 95), which are sometimes decorated in a sober and restrained manner with engraving (Plate 96). Three of v. Eiff's other pupils are working as freelance glass decorators in Stuttgart in original and personal styles: Hanns Model (since 1933), Marianne Schoder (since 1938) and Nora Ortlieb (since 1943). Miss Ortlieb also designs for the Dorotheenhütte, Schwarzwälder Glaswerkstätten. At Zwiesel Rudolf Wagner engraves glass to his own designs.

At the Staatliche Fachschule für Glasindustrie (National Technical College for Glassmaking) at Zwiesel, the traditions of independence and modernism from the past have been continued under the leadership of Max Gangkofner and his staff of teachers, which includes the architect Rudolf Rothemund and Hans Mauder, the son of Bruno Mauder. Of special interest is the glass of Stephan Erdös, who worked as teacher for a time about 1955. His 'folded' pieces especially have a softness and grace which are reminiscent of Gunnel Nyman's work, and which set them apart from glass in the extremely austere style which is most favoured in Germany today.

Holland

The production of art glass at Leerdam has been considerably extended since the war. Two younger men have joined A. D. Copier in the designers' studio: Floris Meydam (b. 1919) came to the factory in 1935, and Willem Heesen (b. 1925) in 1943. This little team has developed a noble genre in art glass, which covers a wide range of techniques and moods, from the dignity of Copier's heavy vases with metallic textural effects (Plate 80B), to the softness and grace of Meydam's furnace-worked models in opal glass (Plate 81A) and Heesen's gaily engraved plaques. To ensure a fine quality of craftsmanship in this latter kind of decoration, a school of engraving has since the war been established at the factory under the leadership of Copier. Cutting has been less extensively used, most interestingly in the rough carved abstract figures which form one of the factory's specialities (Plate 81B). The exquisite quality of the Leerdam crystal is eminently suited to this particular form of glass.

U.S.A.

The Steuben factory at Corning is still the most important industrial maker of art glass in the United States, and the factory's fine soft crystal is being formed into simple furnace-worked shapes (Plate 82A) in the style established there before the war. To stimulate the art of engraving, great artists from many countries have been invited to provide designs. In 1940 twenty-seven painters and sculptors from France, Britain and America were asked to submit designs for engraving; in 1950 a group of famous British artists received a similar invitation, and in 1954 a number of Asian and Near Eastern artists were approached by the Steuben management. The factory's own designers have created shapes to frame the artists' patterns. In some cases it has proved difficult to transfer the ideas of the outside artists to engraving in a fully satisfactory way, while some of the designs were eminently suited to the technique (Plate 83A). None of these schemes has, however, produced any new artistic departure for Steuben. Efforts to produce glass sculpture have sometimes given very interesting results (Plate 83B).

Some good simple models of useful and decorative glass are being produced at the factories of the Blenko Glass Company in West Virginia, where Wayne Husted has been designer since 1953; at the Erickson Glass Works in Bremen, Ohio, to the designs of Carl E. Erickson and Erwin Kalla; at the Libbey Glass Division of the Owens-Illinois Company in Toledo, Ohio, where Freda Diamond is design director, and at the Pilgrim Corporation; the last-named factory was founded by Alfred E. Knobler, who is also its managing director and designer.

The most interesting artistic work in glass in America is being done in private studios. Nestor among American glass decorators is Maurice Heaton (b. 1900), the son of a stained-glass artist in London. Heaton works with flat glass, decorated with enamelling into which he scratches his figures, and which he fires and shapes in the furnace by a technical process of his own invention (Plate 71B). Marianne v. Allesch (b. 1886), formerly a maker of glass figures in Berlin, has designed tableware for various factories in America, and also made some decorative panels with abstract painted decoration. Enamelling on glass is also practised by Eugene M. Winters (b. 1904), an artist of Viennese origin who works in an abstract style, and by the ceramist Earl McCutchen of Georgia, as well as by members of the Glass Guild, Kew Gardens, New York. The Glass Guild was founded in 1953, and here George Briard, Loretta Franceschini (1925–59) and Steven Mildwoff (b. 1940) have decorated blanks from the Pittsburg Plate Glass Company. John Burton of Chatsworth, California, works with coloured glass at the lamp, and Frances and Michael Higgins did decorative work in coloured glass in their own workshop between 1948 and 1958; today they design mainly for the Dearborn Glass Company in Michigan. Priscilla Manning Porter in New York makes some interesting mosaic work in miniature. Edris Eckhardt of Cleveland, Ohio, is an artist in pottery and glass. She does flat and sculptured work in complicated colour techniques, and her experiments into the use of gold and enamels have led to interesting artistic results.

Japan

During the early twentieth century the Japanese produced some pretty engraved glass in the European taste. Since the war, two Japanese factories have begun making some very tasteful versions of the best contemporary Western glass styles in simple and unforced techniques. Kozo Kagami, who in the late 'twenties was a pupil of v. Eiff's in Stuttgart, makes tableware and decorative glass at his factory, the Kagami Crystal Works, in Tokyo. The cheap pressed glass models are of excellent design, while the more elaborate cut glass is less attractive. Masakichi Awashima (b. 1914) was trained at the Design Department of the Art School of Japan. In 1956 he founded his own factory, The Awashima Glass Company, in Tokyo, where he has produced some exquisite models in moulded glass (Plate 80A).

France

The independent glass artist seems to be disappearing in modern France. André Thuret carries on a sporadic production of freely tooled individual pieces, and since the war he has introduced into his work colours and textural effects, obtained through oxidations (Plate 84A). But no young *artistes verriers* have come forward to carry on the great traditions of Rousseau, Brocard and Marinot.

Since the death of René Lalique in 1945, his factory has continued under the leadership of his son Marc Lalique on lines similar to those before the war. The stress is, however, being laid increasingly on glass for interior decoration and architecture, and the production of vessels has become less important. The new style of the factory of Daum was created in 1945 by Michel Daum. From a perfect and brilliant colourless crystal vessels are drawn out into almost abstract shapes through a special furnace technique (Plate 85A); occasionally purely sculptural forms are made (Plate 85B). Modern Daum represents a very high standard of glass-making technique, but the results are sometimes ostentatious and the possibilities of variation are limited. The factory of Baccarat excels as before in elegant and luxurious tableware, and some *tours de force* in brilliant cut glass are made at times (Plate 84B). For Saint-Louis, the designer N. Haesen has created some irregular cut-glass patterns which have a certain intellectual power.

Belgium

The most famous product of the big glass factory of Val-Saint-Lambert is table-glass, but between 1906 and 1959 Charles Graffart designed a series of decorative pieces for the factory, mostly in simple, blown shapes (Plate 77A), and sometimes decorated with cutting and engraving; Graffart followed in a mild way the changing tastes and fashions in the big European centres. He has now been succeeded as head designer by René Delvenne, who has worked in the factory's studio since 1925.

Some interesting things have been produced at the decorating establishment, La Societé Coopérative 'Art et Verre', started in 1945; since 1950 blown glass has also been produced. At the head of the production is Paula Ingrand, who was trained in the highly sophisticated decorating firm of Max Ingrand in Paris.

Britain

After the war the British glass factories have pursued their traditional course, showing up the perfection of lead crystal by means of cut and engraved decoration. The bigger firms now employ professional designers, and generally speaking decoration has been simplified and taste improved.

Geoffrey Baxter (b. 1922) has been resident designer for Whitefriars since 1954. He has absorbed the firm's traditional style of simple, blown forms, and has given it a free and discreetly personal expression, especially in heavy, furnace-worked vases (Plate 86A). He has also struck out a new line in cutting, where the patterns follow the general shape of the vessel.

The firm's managing director, William J. Wilson, continues to design tasteful models in the established style. Some experiments in coloured glass with inlaid air-bubbles are interesting as being the only examples of their kind in the industry in Britain.

R. Stennett-Willson has for many years designed plain, undecorated glass to be executed in Sweden, sometimes in lightly tinted glass. Lately the Lemington factory in Newcastle-on-Tyne has realized his designs.

Since 1946 Irene M. Stevens has been attached to the Stourbridge firm of Webb Corbett and she has done much to introduce softer and gentler lines to both shapes and cut patterns. Some sandblasted models are of a more powerful character (Plate 87A). The designs for cut and engraved glass by Deanne Meanley for Stevens & Williams show a similar tendency towards simplicity and grace. Since 1956 Tom Jones has been the factory's chief designer. John Luxton, who has been attached to Stuart & Sons since 1948, has designed some pretty patterns for engraving. David Hammond works for the Stourbridge firm of Thomas Webb & Sons, and excels in delicate patterns for engraving.

In spite of the improved taste of the English cut-glass production, the makers are still working within exceedingly narrow stylistic limits. The factories will, however, not easily break away from the well-established genre of glass for which there is a large and faithful public both in Britain and abroad, and to the production of which their technical equipment is fitted and their staff trained. In the schools for glassmaking in different parts of Britain, freer scope can be given to experiment. Of the greatest importance are the glass departments at the Royal College of Art in London and at the Stourbridge School of Art, which work in close collaboration.

At the Royal College of Art, which is the main training centre for artist-designers in Britain, Industrial Glass (as opposed to Stained Glass) has been a teaching subject since 1937, and when the College was reorganized in 1949 the department gained considerably in importance. Professor R. Y. Gooden is the head, while William Stanier has been tutor since 1949. Apart from the formal art education to which all students at the College are submitted, the Department of Industrial Glass provides training in engraving, cutting and enamelling, while designs for shapes are executed at the Stourbridge School, which has glass furnaces for crystal and for coloured glass at its disposal. The Glass Department in Stourbridge, which dates from 1934, was moved to the present modern premises in 1956, and apart from the furnaces there is technical equipment for cutting, engraving and sandblasting. The head, J. C. Downing, is himself a graduate from The Royal College of Art. Apart from some high-quality exercises in glass decoration (Plate 87B), the London-Stourbridge partnership has produced some interesting experimental work in coloured and furnace-worked glass (Plate 86B). It seems difficult, however, to exploit in the industry the young talent from the schools.

At the Edinburgh College of Art there has been a Glass Design Department since 1940, from 1947 with Helen Monro Turner as full-time instructor. The Department has technical equipment for engraving, cutting and sandblasting; in 1958 a small furnace was installed for experimental glass, while blown glass is taught on visits to Stourbridge. Mrs. Turner did some designing for the Edinburgh and Leith Flint Glass Works before the war, but her great interest is engraving; from 1938 she studied under v. Eiff in Stuttgart and she has developed a fine individual style in this technique, adapting the classical style taught by v. Eiff to a modern idiom of great purity (Plate 88A). Engravers from many countries have received inspiring training in Edinburgh. In 1956 she established in Edinburgh the Juniper Workshop for glass decoration, where blanks from the factories are bent or cut into shape and decorated with engraving, cutting or sandblasting. Among the young artists who work under Mrs. Turner's inspiring leadership are Marjorie Findlay, John Lawrie, Ronald Renton and Val Rossi; the last-named, who is mainly a furniture designer, works in a highly personal style of a free sculptural character. David Harding is a pupil of Mrs. Turner who has done some independent decorative work.

There is also a flourishing school of free-lance engravers working in various parts of Britain. William J. Wilson at Whitefriars began working with diamond-point engraving in 1935 and he has done much fine and dignified work in this technique, mainly on memorial glass. The most personal of the British glass engravers is Laurence Whistler (b. 1912). During the early 'thirties he amused himself and his friends by scratching lines of poetry on windows in the Elizabethan manner; later he began decorating wineglasses, frequently fine eighteenth-century specimens, with diamond-point line-engraving, each decoration being specially designed for a rich and aristocratic patron. The style of his early work is largely based on the Baroque tradition, with emblems and allegorical allusions as favourite themes. After the war he has mainly been occupied with the exceedingly demanding technique of stipple, and his designs have become personal and imaginative to the point of eccentricity (Plate 89). Most of his glasses are now made to his own designs at Whitefriars. Anthony Pope and Shiela Elmhirst have both done some elegant work in diamond-point, while Stephen Rickard, Dorothy Brown, Harold Gordon and many others do pretty engravings in a gently traditional style. John Hutton (b. New Zealand 1906) has made glass-engraving a monumental art in his large panels for the western front of Coventry Cathedral, where he has obtained fine, light effects by shallow, matted engraving, applied to the glass with a movable wheel. Some of the Coventry figures he has translated on to large vessels, produced by Whitefriars, with very impressive results (Plate 88B).

Bohemia

After the political revolution in Czechoslovakia in 1948, the glass industry was nationalized, and the whole complicated system of factories, decorating centres and teaching institutions was made into one vast organization. In order to bring to fruitful use the immense store of technical knowledge and craftsmanlike skill latent in the country's population, the Creative Glass Centre in Prague was set up in 1952 with the main task of establishing contact between the industry and artists and designers, and of supporting research into new techniques of embellishing glass.

The traditional product of the Bohemian factories is heavily cut crystal, and like its British counterpart and original model, 'Bohemian crystal' still has a large public all over the world. The old rigid cut-glass patterns are, however, gradually going out, and softer patterns of a gently formalized character are being increasingly favoured. Besides the traditional mass production of glass with pretty engraved ornaments, unique pieces with engraving of the finest quality are being made. Jaroslav Horejc continues the magnificent, classical tradition of engraving in his vases with richly varied figure-subjects (Plate 91) from Studio Lobmeyr in the old North-Bohemian 'glass' town of Kamenický Šenov (Steinschönau). It should be mentioned that this establishment has no connection with the Viennese firm of J. & L. Lobmeyr (see p. 63). Věra Lišková (b. 1924) creates fine patterns for engraving on a smaller scale (Plate 90). Furnace-worked glass is also being made in Bohemia. About 1955 glass with inlaid coloured stripes, the so-called 'Harrtil' glass, was first made at the old Harrachov works according to a process newly invented by the factory's manager, Miloš Půlpitel. The basic idea has been developed on more imaginative lines (Plate 93A). The freely furnace-worked glass made by Emanuel Beránek at the Škrdlovice factory and by František Zemek at the Palme König factory is technically skilful, but without genuine feeling for form, and the varieties made with colours or inlaid bubbles can be criticized on the same score. Zemek's glass leopard (Plate 92), exhibited at the Milan Triennale in 1957, is a striking piece.

As in Britain, the most interesting work in Bohemia is being done by students, who can experiment more freely than designers working for the industry. Some very interesting results of experiments at the Prager Kunstgewerbeschule (School of Applied Arts) were shown at the Milan Triennale in 1957 and 1960. There was glass in simple, massive forms (Plate 93B), and glass with inlaid colours as well as acid-engraved, wheel-engraved and cut glass; Finland and Sweden had obviously provided important inspiration, while v. Eiff's influence could be distinguished in some of the engraved work. In the School the modern direction is being followed up, but the influence of this interesting work on the industry is as yet not very marked.

GLASS AND THE ARTIST

In the previous pages we have studied the development of art glass over a period of almost a hundred years, and we have discussed the *œuvre* of more than seventy glass artists at forty or fifty factories in thirteen different countries. In spite of the great variety of techniques and of personal and national styles in our material, the period has certain characteristic features, which make it natural to consider it as a unity within the history of art glass.

First, it has been *the age of colour-glass*. We have seen how the technical knowledge of colour in glass, which was developed during the Romantic period, provided the background for the products of Rousseau, Gallé, Tiffany and their contemporaries – the first art glass in our modern sense of the word. Much excellent work was done during the period that followed – in engraving (at Orrefors, Lobmeyr's and Steuben, and by v. Eiff and his pupils), in cutting (especially at Kosta and Orrefors and by the British firm of Stevens & Williams), as well in 'simple pieces'[1] (at Strömsbergshyttan, Whitefriars and Steuben). But it was undoubtedly in complicated colour techniques that the most imaginative and original work was done – by Marinot and his followers in France, by Simon Gate, Edward Hald and their school in Sweden; while in Murano the colour techniques traditional to the island were employed in a highly characteristic, contemporary idiom by Venini and Ercole Barovier, so that Venetian glass became one of the most truly modern creations of their time.

[1] The expression is borrowed from R. Stennett-Willson, who uses it in his book, *The Beauty of Modern Glass* (London 1958), to describe plain, undecorated pieces of transparent glass.

The glassmakers in Murano are not likely materially to change their stylistic course, which has four hundred years of continuous tradition behind it, but in Northern Europe and in America there are signs that the present age of colour-glass is drawing towards its close. Much excellent colour-glass is still being made, especially in Sweden, Norway and Holland. But young glass designers in Scandinavia, in Germany and in America are increasingly concentrating on shape at the cost of textural effects. At the exhibition in Munich in 1959 simple, neatly shaped glasses with distinctive profiles prevailed, produced by blowing into a mould lightweight material, sometimes of a single subtle colour.

Our period has also been *the age of the glass artist.* (In English the expression is strange and awkward, whereas the French *artiste verrier* and the German *Glaskünstler* have long been accepted.) We have seen how he emerged in France during the latter part of the nineteenth century, and how the ambition to make glassmaking an art, on a par with painting and sculpture, has inspired producers of glass in many countries to their finest achievements. The glass artist could be one of many things. Glassmaking is not normally a personal craft, but an industry carried out in a factory, and the making of a single piece involves a number of different professionals; the artistic impulse has come – at different times and in different countries – from each of the individual links in the chain of collaboration. In the course of technical work in the laboratory Edvard Strömberg in Sweden and Hugo Debach in Germany were inspired to develop forms and techniques which showed off the beauties of the material they had created. Glassblowers like Knut Bergqvist in Sweden, Arturo Biasiutto in Murano and Tom Hill in London have been stimulated to creative work while collaborating with the designer; whilst independent artists like Marinot, Sala and Thuret have worked out their ideas in person at the furnace. Decorators in many fields have enhanced the beauty of glass by adding ornamentation in various techniques, and the best of them, such as Brocard, the Lobmeyr engravers, v. Eiff and Laurence Whistler, have also designed the shape of the glass they were to decorate, so that form and *décor* became one. And the head of a factory can at times direct and inspire his whole team of technicians, craftsmen and decorators to execute his personal ideas, as happened in the case of Gallé and Tiffany, Lalique and Venini.

Since the First World War the aesthetic side of glass production in Northern Europe and in the U.S.A. has been increasingly delegated to designers, who stand outside the actual production. The first generation of this category of glass artists was trained in other artistic fields: Gate and

Hald were painters, Jacob Bang, Keith Murray and John Monteith Gates were architects. Today their task is being taken over by professional industrial designers, and this may account to some extent both for the general high standard of taste and style in contemporary glass and the simplicity of techniques used. Some industrial designers, who work with equal ease in many materials, have produced excellent glass, such as Wirkkala and Sarpaneva in Finland and Bongard and Jutrem in Norway. At times, however, one feels that their creations are products of the drawing-board rather than of a deep and excited experience of glass, and that the field of glass design is becoming dangerously narrowed down. The progressive style of today gives little scope for personal and imaginative work. However one may admire the shapeliness of the products of the younger generation and the unforced simplicity both in material and workmanship, one cannot help feeling that they betray a somewhat narrow conception of glass as a material, and that the possibilities of variation are very limited. We look forward to the time when artists will again apply the full force of their talents to the understanding of glass and the exploration of its aesthetic potentialities, and give us fully orchestrated symphonies, not merely chamber music.

SIGNATURES

MODERN = in use today

v. Allesch. 1948.

Baccarat. Stamped and etched. Modern.

BRIERLEY — Brierley. Stamped and etched. Modern.

Angelo Barovier Murano 60 — Barovier, Angelo. Diamond-engraved on specially good pieces. Modern.

de Bazel. 1924. After Pazaurek: Kunstgläser. Similar mark in use today.

HB — Bongard. Diamond-engraved with *Hadeland* on every piece made to his design and with a number in the 1000 series. Modern.

Brocard. Enamelled in red. 1878. Pl. 14. A piece from 1885 in Musée des Arts Décoratifs is signed in gold 'Brocard & Fils, Paris'.

SB — Brörby. Diamond-engraved with *Hadeland* on every piece made to his design with a number in the 7000 series. Modern.

Copier. Engraved on every piece of 'Unica' glass made to his design with number and date-letter. Modern.

B — Cyrén. Diamond-engraved on every piece of engraved glass made to his design, with *Orrefors* or *Of*.

BA — Cyrén. Ditto on cut glass.

BU — Cyrén. Ditto on furnace-worked glass.

Dammouse. Impressed on every piece. S = Sèvres.

DAUM NANCY — Daum. Engraved and gilt, 1900. Pl. 9 a.

Daum Nancy — Daum. Gilt, early 20th century. R. Scott. Mus. 1958-157.

Daum France — Daum. Stamped and etched. Modern.

Décorchemont. Impressed on every piece.

Drahoňovsky. 1924. After Pazaurek: Kunstgläser.

W.v.E v. Eiff. 1924. After Pazaurek: Kunstgläser.

Farquharson. Etched, 1939. Pl. 59 a.

Franck. Diamond-engraved. Modern.

Gallé. Enamelled in red. *c.* 1889. R. Scott. Mus. 1892-518.

Gallé. Engraved. *c.* 1889. R. Scott. Mus. 1892-516.

Gallé. Engraved. *c.* 1889. Pl. 9 b. and colour plate A.

Gallé. In relief on the side. Pl. 10

Gallé. Engraved. 1889. Pl. 11 b.

Gallé. Etched. *c.* 1900. Mrs. G. Gros.

Gallé. Etched. Perhaps after 1904. V & A. C. 1243-1917.

Gallé. Etched. Pl. 12 and 13.

Gate. Engraved. Graal glass, 1917. KB = Knut Bergqvist. Bergen, Kunstindustrimuseum.

G Gate. Diamond-engraved on every piece of engraved glass made to his design, with *Orrefors* or *Of.* Modern.

GA	Gate. Ditto on cut glass.
GU	Gate. Ditto on furnace-worked glass.
Hd-KB	Hald. Diamond-engraved on engraved glass, 1917. KB = Knut Bergqvist. Bergen, Kunstindustrimuseum.
Graal Orrefors 1917 KB - HW N:425.	Hald. Diamond-engraved on Graal glass, 1917. KB = Knut Bergqvist. Bergen, Kunstindustrimuseum.
H	Hald. Diamond-engraved on every piece of engraved glass made to his design, with *Orrefors* or *Of*. Modern.
HA	Hald. Ditto on cut glass.
HU	Hald. Ditto on furnace-worked glass.
M.H.	Heaton. On every piece. Modern.
H	Heesen. On every piece of 'Unica' glass made to his designs with number and date-letter. Modern.
JH	Hidle. Diamond-engraved with *Hadeland* on every piece made to his design with a number in the 5000 series. Modern.
JWJ	Johansson, Wilhelm. Diamond-engraved with *Hadeland* on every piece made to his design and with a number in the 3000 series. Modern.
WJ	Johansson, Willy. Diamond-engraved with *Hadeland* on every piece made to his design and with a number in the 2000 series. Modern.
AJ	Jutrem. Diamond-engraved with *Hadeland* on every piece made to his design and with a number in the 4000 series. Modern.
R Lalique	Lalique. Engraved. 1924. V. & A. C.1499 a–1924.
Lalique	Lalique. Seal stamp. 1924. V. & A. C.1496–1924.
R LALIQUE FRANCE	Lalique. Engraved. *c.* 1930. Pl. 31 a.
Lalique France	Lalique. Stamped and etched. Modern.
N	Landberg. Diamond-engraved on every piece of engraved glass made to his design, with *Orrefors* or *Of*. Modern.
NA	Landberg. Ditto on cut glass.
NU	Landberg. Ditto on furnace-worked glass.
L	Lindstrand at Orrefors. Diamond-engraved on every piece of engraved glass made to his design, with *Orrefors* or *Of*. Modern.

LA — Lindstrand. Ditto on cut glass.

LU — Lindstrand. Ditto on furnace-worked glass.

Lobmeyr. Engraved on important pieces after 1860. After Pazaurek: Kunstgläser. Modern.

de Lorm. 1924. After Pazaurek: Kunstgläser.

D — Lundin. Diamond-engraved on every piece of engraved glass made to her design, with *Orrefors* or *Of*. Modern.

DA — Lundin. Ditto on cut glass.

DU — Lundin. Ditto on furnace-worked glass.

LÜTKEN — Lütken. Every piece made to his design signed with his name and date. Modern.

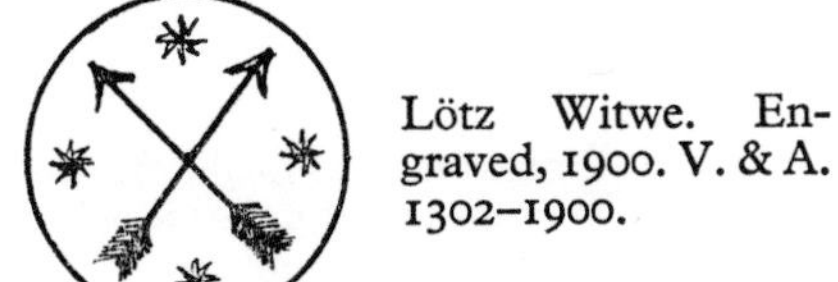

Lötz Witwe. Engraved, 1900. V. & A. 1302–1900.

Marinot. Etched on every piece.

M — Meydam. On every piece of 'Unica' glass made to his design, with number and date-letter. Modern.

Monro. Diamond-engraved in recent pieces.

Keith Murray BRIERLEY — Murray. Stamped and etched.

P — Palmqvist. Diamond-engraved on every piece of engraved glass made to his design, with *Orrefors* or *Of*. Modern.

PA — Palmqvist. Ditto on cut glass.

PU — Palmqvist. Ditto on furnace-worked glass.

SP — Pettersen. Engraved on important pieces.

E Rousseau Paris — Rousseau. Engraved with gilt flourish. Prob. 1885. Pl.2 17, R. Scott Mus.

E. Léveillé E Rousseau Paris. 74 Bd Haussmann

Rousseau-Léveillé. Léveillé's name and address added to Rousseau's signature in diamond-engraving. Pl. 2, V. 2A.

J. Sala	Sala. On every piece.
TIMO SARPANEVA IITTALA	Sarpaneva. Engraved, with date, on every piece made to his design.
ÅVS 1959	Schrader. Diamond-engraved on important pieces.
C	Selbing. Diamond-engraved on every piece of engraved glass made to his design, with *Orrefors* or *Of*. Modern.
CA	Selbing. Ditto on cut glass.
CU	Selbing. Ditto on furnace-worked glass.
Steuben 1939	Steuben. Engraved. 1939. Pl. 82 b.
STEUBEN	Steuben. Diamond-engraved in cursive script on every piece. Modern.
Stuart ENGLAND	Stuart and Sons. Stamped and etched. Modern.
ANDRÉ THURET	Thuret. Diamond-engraved on every piece.
Louis C. Tiffany L.C.T	Tiffany. Engraved. 1899. Pl. 19 a.
venini murano ITALIA	Venini. Stamped and etched. Modern.
MADE IN Webb ENGLAND	Thos. Webb & Sons. Stamped and etched. Modern.
Webb	
WEBB CORBETT S ENGLAND	Webb Corbett. Stamped and etched. With S, made at Stourbridge factory. With T, made at Tutbury factory. Modern.
LW 1960	Whistler. Diamond-engraved with date on every recent piece. Double size.
TAPIO WIRKKALA - IITTALA	Wirkkala. Engraved, with date, on every piece made to his design. Modern.
F	Öhrström. Diamond-engraved on every piece of engraved glass made to his design with *Orrefors* or *Of*.
FA	Öhrström. Ditto on cut glass
FU	Öhrström. Ditto on furnace-worked glass.

SELECT BIBLIOGRAPHY

Yolande Amic, *L'opaline française au XIXe siècle*, Paris (1952).

L. M. Angus-Butterworth, *British Table and Ornamental Glass*, London (1956).

James Barrelet, *La verrerie en France de l'époque gallo-romaine à nos jours*, Paris (1953).

Louis de Forcaud, *Emile Gallé*, Paris (1903).

Larry Freeman, *Iridescent Glass*, New York (1956).

Emile Gallé, *Écrits pour l'art*, Paris (1908).

Astone Gasparetto, *Il vetro di Murano dalle origini ad oggi*, Venezia (1958).

H. E. van Gelder, 'Modern European Glass', *Encyclopædia Britannica*, London and New York (1929).

Gabriella Gros, 'Poetry in Glass. The Art of Emile Gallé', *Apollo* (November 1955).

Guillaume Janneau, *Le verre et l'art de Marinot*, Paris (1925).

Guillaume Janneau, *Modern Glass*, London and New York (1931).

Oili Mäki, *Finnish Designers of To-day*, Helsinki (1954).

Giovanni Mariacher, *L'arte del vetro* (1954).

Helen Monro, 'Glass Engraving', *The Studio* (October 1960).

Keith Murray, 'The Design of Table Glass', *Design for To-day* (June 1933).

William B. O'Neal, 'Three *Art Nouveau* Glass Makers', *Journal of Glass Studies*, Vol. II, Corning Glass Center, New York (1960).

Nora Ortlieb, *Wilhelm von Eiff*, Bamberg (1950).

Gustav E. Pazaurek, *Moderne Gläser*, Leipzig n.d. (1901).

Gustav E. Pazaurek, *Kunstgläser der Gegenwart*, Leipzig (1925).

James S. Plaut, *Steuben Glass*, 2nd ed., New York (1951).

Ada Polak, 'Edward Hald and Orrefors', *The Norseman* (1955).

Léon Rosenthal, *La verrerie française depuis cinquante ans*, Paris and Bruxelles (1927).

Robert Schmidt, *100 Jahre österreichische Glaskunst: 1823 Lobmeyr 1923*, Wien (1925).

Elisa Steenberg, *Modern Swedish Glass*, Stockholm (1949).

R. Stennett-Willson, *The Beauty of Modern Glass*, London and New York (1958).

Valentine van Tassel, 'Louis Comfort Tiffany. I. Favrile Glass. II. Tiffany Products', *The Antiques Journal* (July and August 1952).

Tiffany Glass and Decorating Company, *Tiffany favrile glass considered in its chronological relationship to other glass, as well as its usefulness in the decorative arts*, New York (1896).

Hugh Wakefield, 'Modern Glass from 1850', *Encyclopædia Britannica*, London (1957).

Laurence Whistler, *The Engraved Glass of Laurence Whistler*, London (1952).

Laurence Whistler, *Engraved Glass, 1952-58*, London (1959).

SOME IMPORTANT EXHIBITION CATALOGUES

The Exhibits of Louis C. Tiffany from the Tiffany Studios, Paris (1900).

The Collection of Designs by Twenty-seven Contemporary Artists, Steuben Glass, New York (1940).

L'art du verre, Musée des Arts Décoratifs, Paris (juin-juillet 1951).

Modern Art in Finland, London (The Arts Council) (1953).

British Artists in Crystal, Steuben Glass, New York (1954).

Asian Artists in Crystal, Steuben Glass, New York (1956).

Louis Comfort Tiffany, Museum of Contemporary Crafts, New York (1958).

Trois millénaires d'art verrier à travers les collections publiques et privées de Belgique, Musée Curtius, Liège (1958).

Aspects de la verrerie contemporaine, Musée Curtius, Liège (1958).

Glass 1959, The Corning Museum of Glass, Corning, New York (1959).

Vetri di Murano 1860–1960, Palazzo della Gran Guardia, Verona (March 1960).

INDEX

PLATES

1. *Cased-glass vase, by Rousseau,* 1885. *Ht.* 6¼ *in.*
Musée des Arts Décoratifs, Paris
(*See page* 22)

2. *Engraved and gilt vase, by Rousseau-Léveillé,* 1885. *Ht.* $8\frac{1}{2}$ *in. Royal Scottish Museum, Edinburgh. Another in Victoria and Albert Museum*
(*See pages* 22, 23, 87)

3. *'The Bamboo Vase', engraved and enamelled, by Rousseau,* 1878. *Ht.* 10½ *in.*
Musée des Arts Décoratifs, Paris
(*See page* 22)

4. *Jug with mauve colour-streaks, by Rousseau, 1885. Ht. 9 in.*
Conservatoire National des Arts et Métiers, Paris
(See page 22)

5. *Vase with lacquer-red colour-streaks, by Rousseau, c.* 1885. *Ht.* 8 *in.*
Musée des Arts Décoratifs, Paris
(*See page* 22)

6. *Vase of smoke-coloured glass, by A. Jean, c.* 1890. *Ht.* 19¼ *in.*
Conservatoire National des Arts et Métiers, Paris
(*See page* 32)

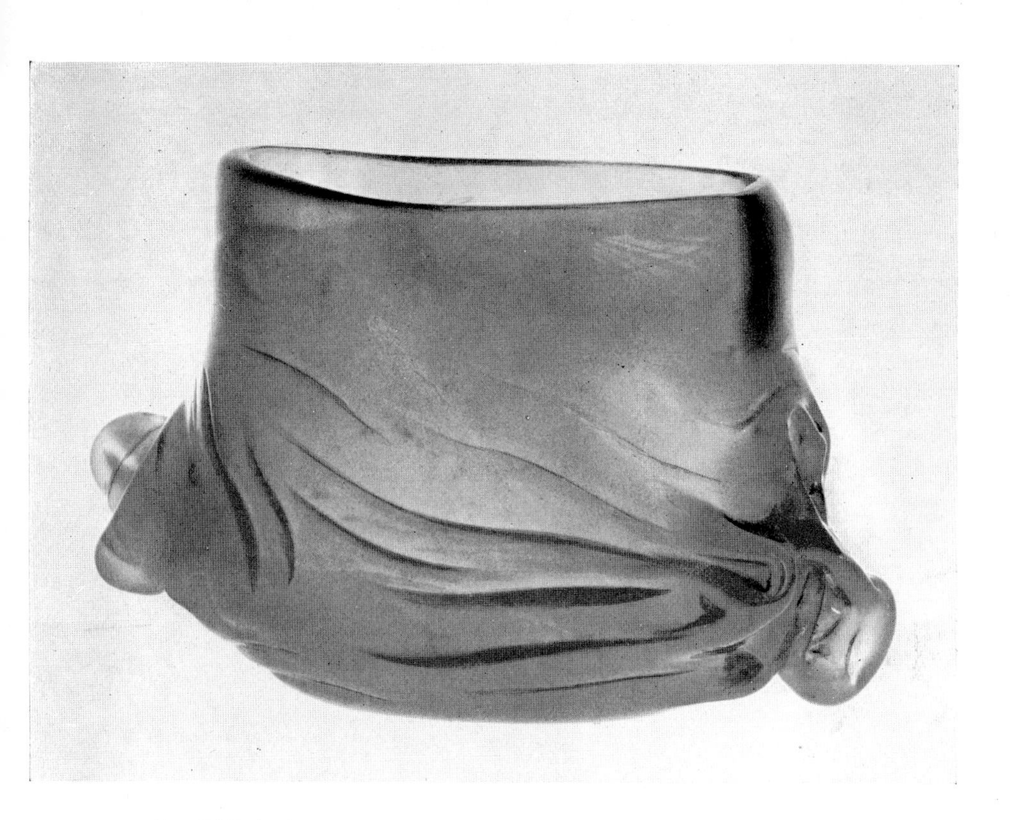

7A. *Vase of jade-coloured glass, by Léveillé,* 1900.
Kunstindustrimuseum, Copenhagen
(*See page* 23)
7B. *Vase of opaque brown glass, by Léveillé, c.* 1890. *Ht.* 6¼ *in.*
Victoria and Albert Museum
(*See page* 23)

8A. *'La Libellule', by Gallé, c.* 1900. *Ht.* $7\frac{7}{8}$ *in. Conservatoire National des Arts et Métiers, Paris*
(*See pages* 27, 29)

8B. *'Porte-cigare', by Gallé,* 1884. *Ht.* $3\frac{5}{8}$ *in. Musée des Arts Décoratifs, Paris*
(*See page* 24)

. *Vase with cloudy red, white*
d green pattern, by Daum,
1900. *Ht.* 6½ *in.*
ordenfjeldske Kunstindustri-
museum, Trondheim
(*See pages* 31, 84)

9B. *Vase, enamelled in black, red*
and gold, by Gallé, 1889.
Ht. 4⅝ *in.*
Victoria and Albert Museum
(*See pages* 24, 28, 85)

10. *'The Oak Vase', cased glass, by Gallé, c.* 1890. *Ht.* 10 *in.*
Victoria and Albert Museum
(*See pages* 27, 29, 85)

11A. *Cased-glass vase in aubergine, brown and white, by Gallé,* 1890–1900. *Corning Museum of Glass, New York* (*See pages* 27, 29)

11B. '*Verrerie parlaute*' *in blue and white cased glass, by Gallé,* 1889. *Ht.* $5\frac{1}{4}$ *in. Musée des Arts Décoratifs, Paris* (*See pages* 24, 25, 85)

12. *Green, frosted flacon with enamelled motif, by Gallé,* 1900. *Ht.* 6 *in. Mrs. Gabriella Gros, London. Another in Vestlandske Kunstindustrimuseum, Bergen*
(*See pages* 28, 29, 85)

13. *Green, frosted vase with enamelled motif, by Gallé,* 1900. *Ht.* $5\frac{1}{4}$ *in.*
Mrs. Ada Polak, London
(*See pages* 28, 29, 85)

14. *Tazza with enamelled pattern, by Brocard,* 1878. *Diam.* 12½ *in.*
Royal Scottish Museum, Edinburgh
(*See page* 32)

15A. *Bowl of opalescent glass with enamelled decoration of mistletoe, by Brocard, c.* 1885. *Ht.* 4½ *in.*
Musée des Arts Décoratifs, Paris
(*See page* 32)

15B. *Bowl of opalescent glass with enamelled decoration of 'monnaie du pape', by Brocard, c.* 1885. *Ht.* 3¼ *in.*
Musée des Arts Décoratifs, Paris
(*See page* 32)

16. *Vase, pâte de verre, by Dammouse,* 1902. *Ht.* 4¾ *in.*
Musée des Arts Décoratifs, Paris
(*See page* 33)

17. *Vase, pâte de verre, by Décorchemont, c.* 1910. *Ht.* 7 *in.*
Musée des Arts Décoratifs, Paris
(*See page* 33)

18. *Engraved beaker, model by Rousseau,* 1885, *produced by Léveillé,* 1890.
Ht. 18 *in.*
Victoria and Albert Museum
(*See page* 22)

19A. *Blue-green, iridescent vase with gold leaves, by Tiffany, 1899. Ht.* $7\frac{3}{4}$ *in.*
Victoria and Albert Museum
(*See pages* 36, 88)

19B. *Peacock-coloured, iridescent bowl, by Tiffany,* 1896. *Ht.* $3\frac{7}{8}$ *in.*
Royal Scottish Museum, Edinburgh
(*See page* 35)

20. *Iridescent vase, with peacock-pattern, by Tiffany,* 1896. *Ht.* 14⅛ *in.*
Courtesy of The Metropolitan Museum of Art, New York
(*Gift of H. O. Havemeyer,* 1896)
(*See pages* 35, 36)

21A. *Iridescent bowl with white line-patterns, by Tiffany,* 1897. *Ht.* 4 *in.*
Nordenfjeldske Kunstindustrimuseum, Trondheim
(*See pages* 35, 36)
21B. *Iridescent bowl with indents, by Tiffany,* 1896.
Courtesy of The Metropolitan Museum of Art, New York
(*Gift of H. O. Havemeyer,* 1896)
(*See page* 37)

22. *Acid-etched vase, by Marinot, c.* 1920. *Ht.* 10¾ *in.*
Musée des Arts Décoratifs, Paris
(*See page* 41)

23. *Enamelled vase, by Marinot, c.* 1920. *Ht.* $13\frac{1}{2}$ *in.*
Musée Galliéra, Paris
(*See page* 40)

24A. *Acid-etched flacon, by Marinot, c.* 1935.
M. Pierre Lévy, Troyes
(*See page* 40)

24B. *Grey-yellow bowl with inlaid bubbles, by Marinot, c.* 1935.
Collection Marinot, Troyes
(*See page* 41)

25A. *Light-blue flacon with inlaid bubbles, by Marinot, 1934.* *Ht.* $7\frac{1}{2}$ *in.* *Musée des Arts Décoratifs, Paris* (*See page* 41)

25B. *Flacon with inlaid colours, by Marinot, c.* 1935. *Collection Marinot, Troyes* (*See page* 41)

26A. *Blue vase, Daum, 1925. Ht. 5⅜ in. Musées Royaux d'Art et d'Histoire, Brussels*
(*See page* 44)

26B. *Grey vase with inlaid patterns, by Navarre, c. 1930. Ht. 8¾ in. Victoria and Albert Museum*
(*See page* 43)

27A. *Grey vase with green leaves, by Sala,* 1929. *Ht.* 12 *in.*
(*See page* 43)

27B. *Pale green vase, by Thuret,* 1930–35.
André Thuret, Paris
(*See page* 43)

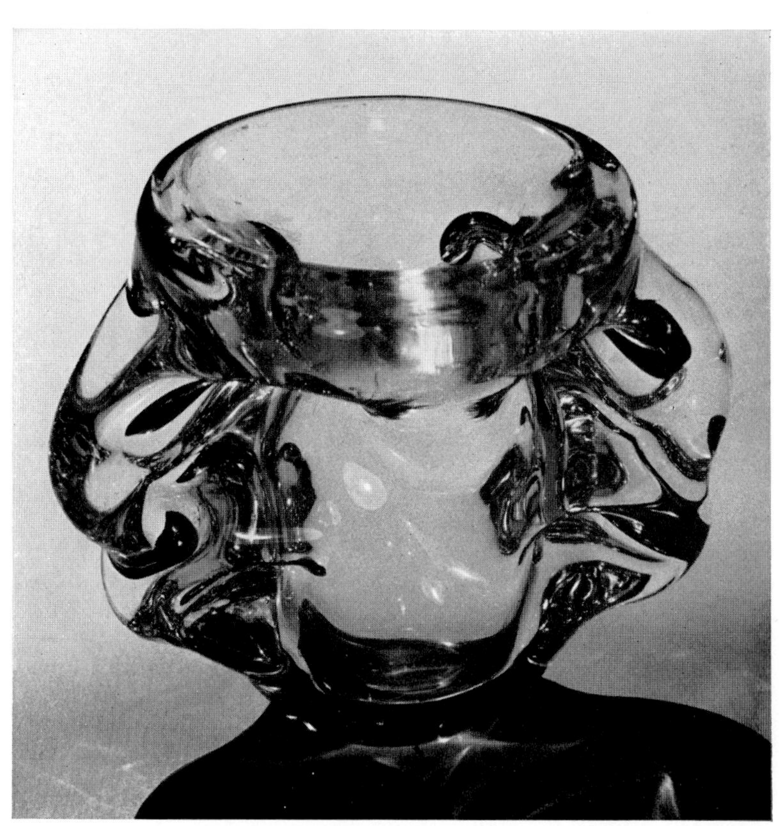

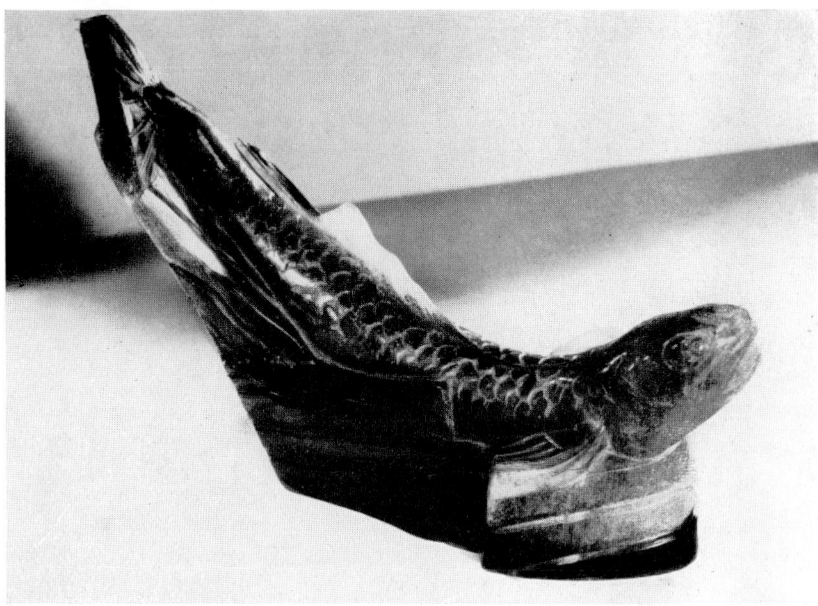

28A. *Vase, green pâte de verre, by Décorchemont,* 1930. *Ht.* $6\frac{3}{8}$ *in.*
Royal Scottish Museum, Edinburgh
(*See page* 43)

28B. *Fish, grey and pink pâte de verre, by Décorchemont,* 1949.
(*See page* 43)

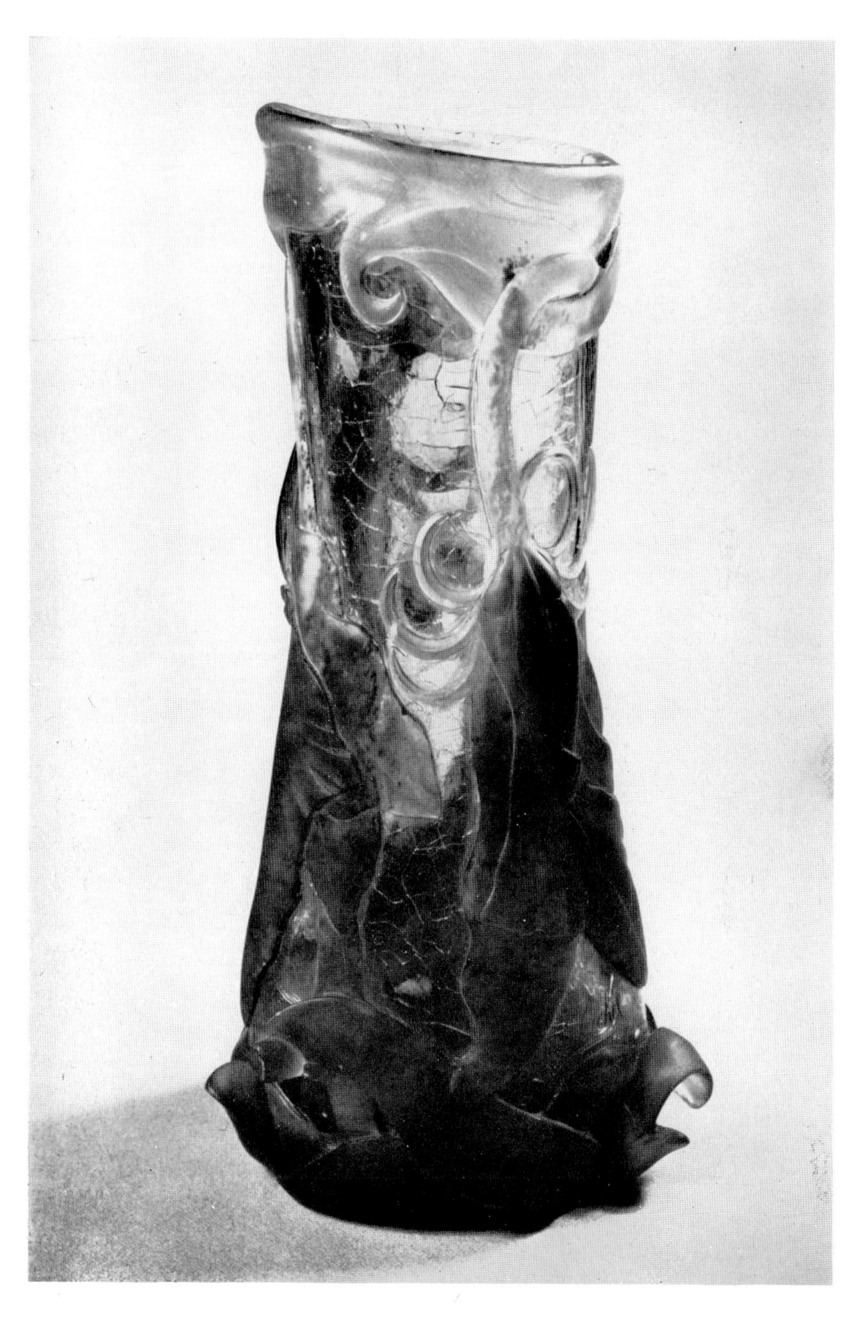

29. *Vase of brown and amethyst glass, by Michel, c.* 1900. *Ht.* $8\frac{5}{8}$ *in.*
Musée des Arts Décoratifs, Paris
(*See page* 23)

30A. *Moulded vase, by Lalique, c.* 1925. *Ht.* $10\frac{1}{2}$ *in.*
Musée des Arts Décoratifs, Paris
(*See page* 45)
30B. *Moulded vases with cocks, by Lalique, c.* 1925.
(*See page* 45)

31A. *Moulded vase with opalescent leaves, by Lalique, c. 1930.*
Baroness Hermione Cederstrom, London
(*See pages* 45, 85)

[3]1B. *Moulded vase, by* [L]*alique, 1925. Ht.* $7\frac{3}{4}$ *in.* [K]*unstindustrimuseum, Co*[pe]*nhagen. Copies in other collections*
(*See page* 45)

32. *'Graal glass no. 1', by Gate, Orrefors, 1916.*
Orrefors Museum
(*See page* 48)

33. *'Girls playing ball'*, *by Hald, Orrefors*, 1919.
(*See page* 49)

34. *Goblet of grey-brown glass, by Gate, Orrefors,* 1923.
(*See page* 48)

35. *Vase on a black foot, by Gate, Orrefors,* 1930.
(*See page* 48)

36. *Graal glass with figures, by Gate, Orrefors,* 1917.
Vestlandske Kunstindustrimuseum, Bergen
(*See page* 48)

37. *Graal glass with mauve line-pattern, by Hald, Orrefors,* 1917.
Vestlandske Kunstindustrimuseum, Bergen
(*See page* 48)

38. *Cut-glass vase, by Elis Bergh, Kosta,* 1931.
(*See page* 49)

39. *'Fireworks', engraved vase, by Hald, Orrefors*, 1921.
(*See page* 49)

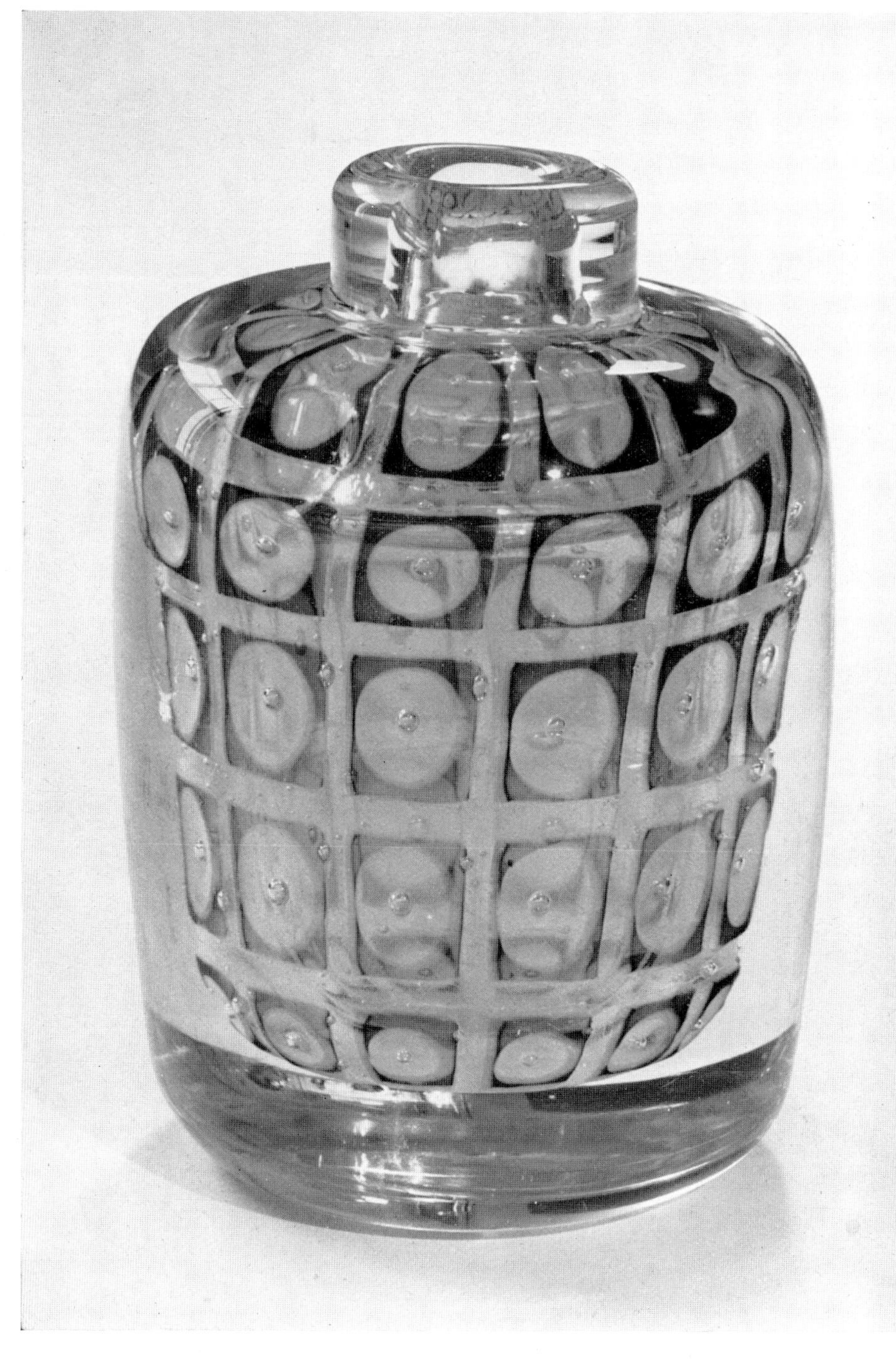

40. *Graal glass with pink inlay, by Hald, Orrefors, 1937. Mrs. Elisa Hald Steenberg, Stockholm*

(*See page* 50)

41. *Engraved vase, by Gate, Orrefors*, 1929.
(*See page* 49)

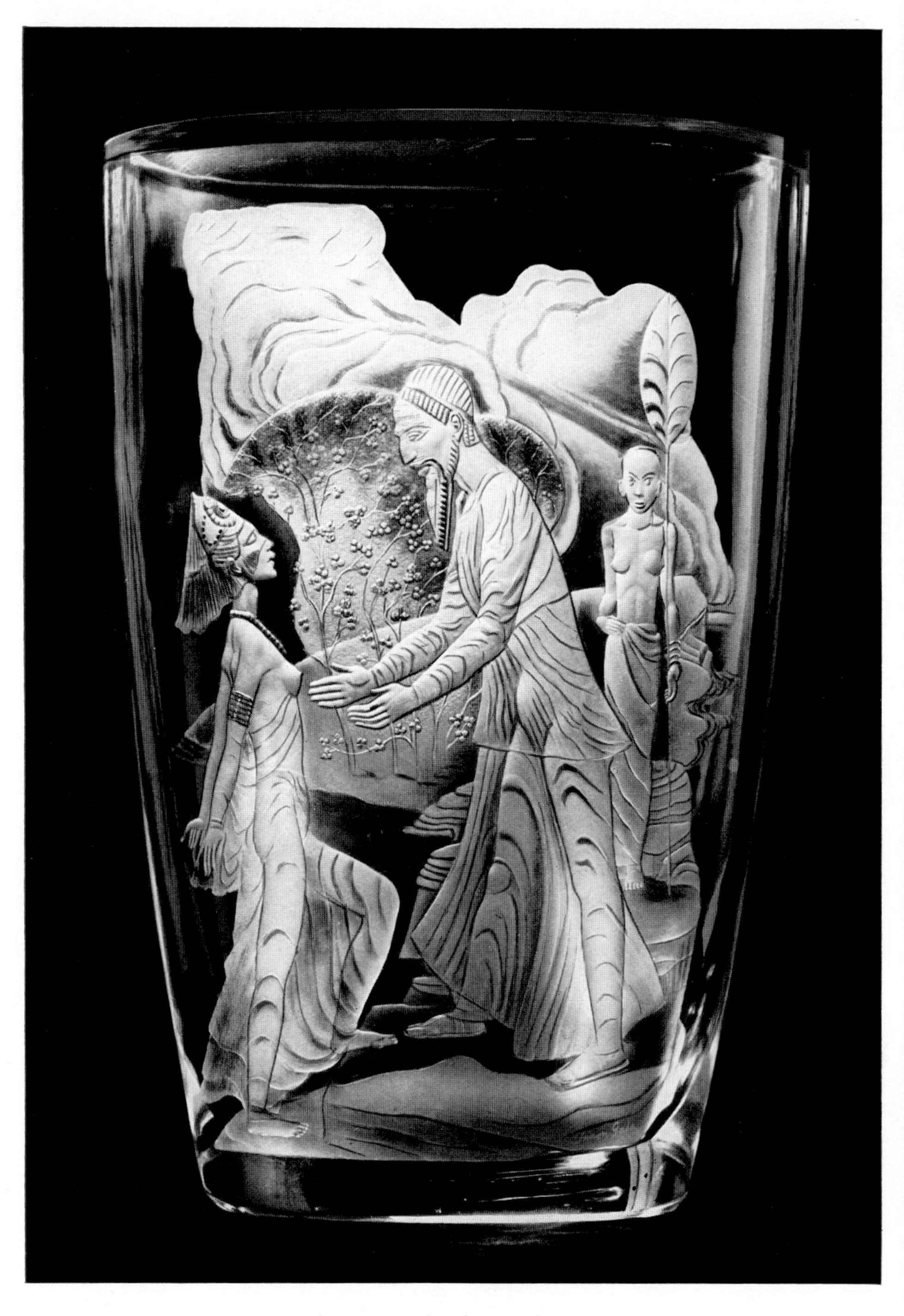

42. *'King Solomon and the Queen of Sheba'*, *by Gate, Orrefors*, 1938.
(*See page* 50)

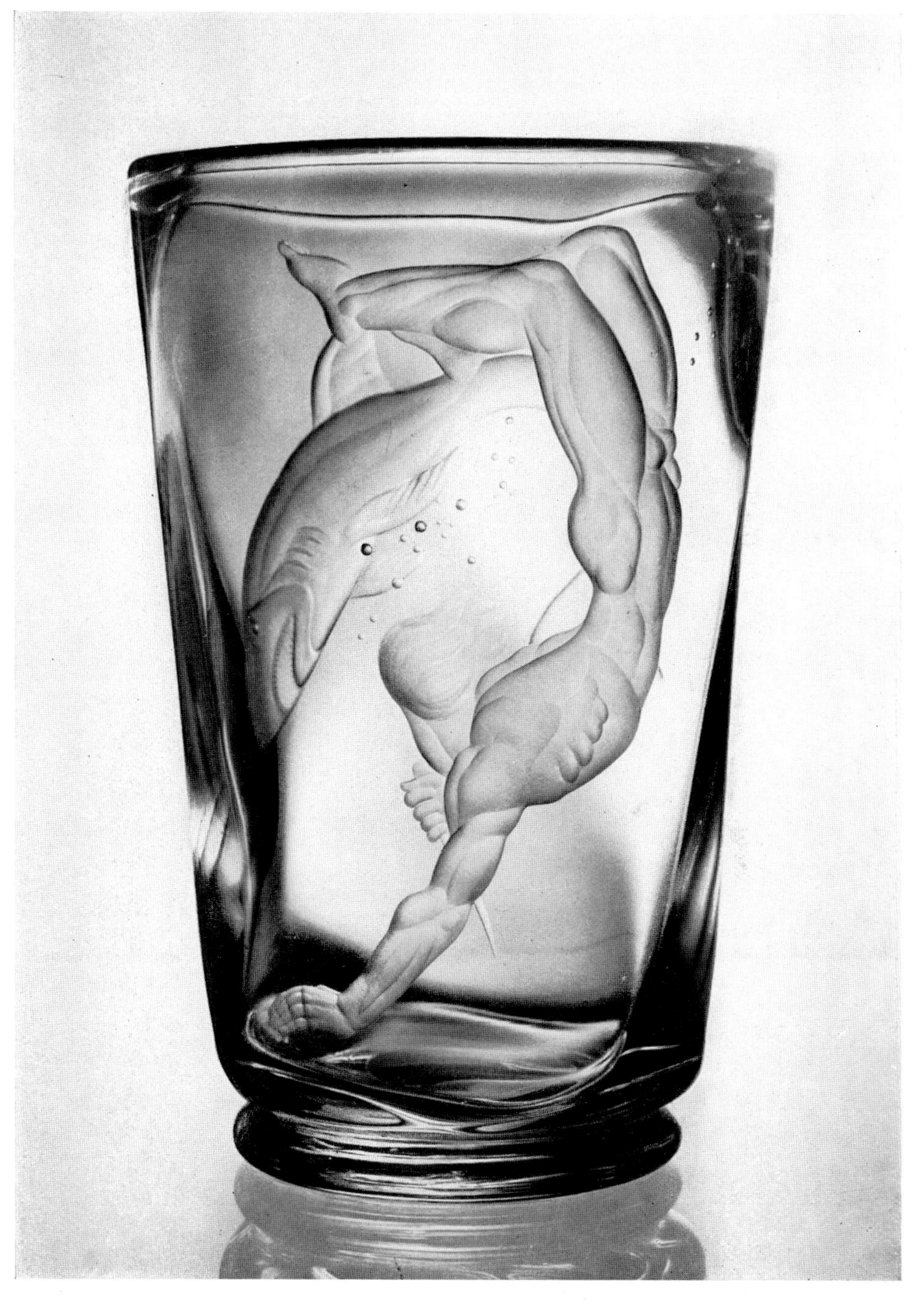

43. *'The Shark-killer', by Lindstrand, Orrefors,* 1937.
(*See page* 50)

44. *Ariel-vase with dark green inlay, by Öhrström, Orrefors, 1939. Nationalmuseum, Stockholm*
(*See page* 50)

45. *Ariel-vase with brown and opaque-white inlay, by Lindstrand, Orrefors*, 1938.
(*See page* 50)

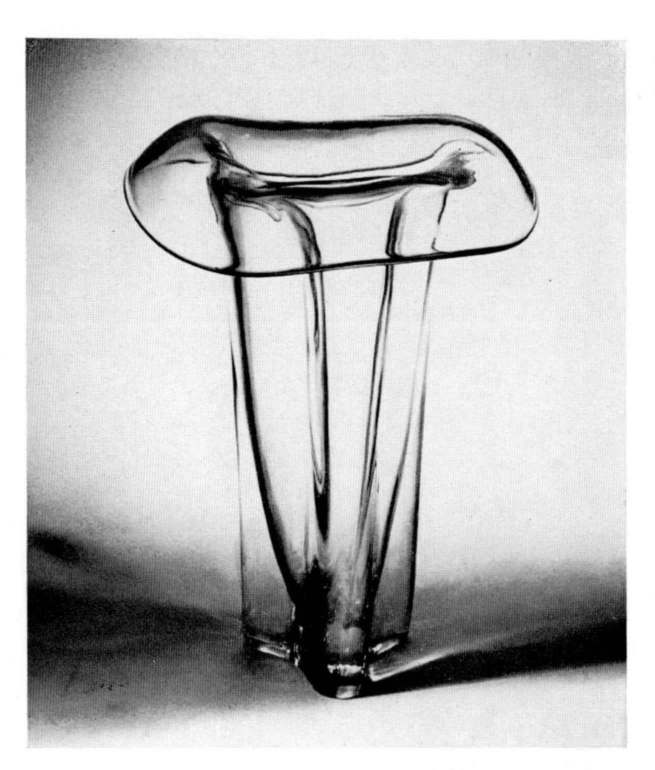

46A. *Vase by Arttu Brummer, Riihimäki, c.* 1930–40. (*See page* 52)

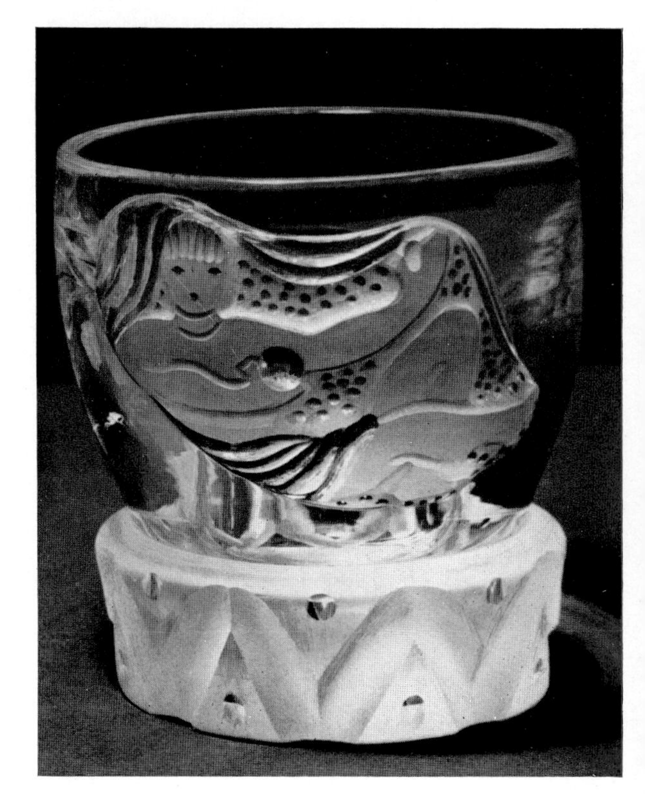

46B. *Engraved and sand-blasted vase, by Pettersen, Hadeland,* 1938. *Kunstindustrimuseum, Oslo* (*See page* 51)

47A. *Vase of green glass, by Alvar Aalto, Karhula-Iittala,* 1938. *Kunstindustrimuseum, Oslo*
(*See page* 52)

47B. *Vase designed by Bang, engraved by Runemalm, c.* 1940. *Kunstindustrimuseum, Copenhagen*
(*See page* 51)

48. *'Ikora'-glass, Württembergische Metallwarenfabrik, c.* 1930.
(*See page* 54)

49A. *'Ikora'-vase, Württemburgische Metallwarenfabrik,* 1930. *Ht.* 3½ *in.*
Nordenfjeldske Kunstindustrimuseum, Trondheim
(*See page* 54)
49B. *Black mottled vase, by Lebeau, Leerdam,* 1923. *Ht.* 9¼ *in.*
Nordenfjeldske Kunstindustrimuseum, Trondheim
(*See page* 53)

50A. *Vetri sommersi, by Venini,* 1934.
(*See page* 56)
50B. *Millefiori dish, by Salviati, c.* 1880. *Diam.* 7 *in.*
Royal Scottish Museum, Edinburgh
(*See page* 54)

51A. *Small bowl in vetro corroso, by Venini, 1933.*
(*See page* 56)

51B. *Vases in shapes derived from glass in pictures by Veronese and Holbein.*
Cappellin-Venini, 1921–24.
(*See page* 55)

52. *Plant in vetro pulegoso, designed by Martinuzzi for Venini, 1928.*
(*See page* 56)

53A. *Jug in primavera glass, by Ercole Barovier,* 1927.
(*See page* 57)
53B. *Dish, engraved by Pelzel to the design of Balsamo Stella,* 1922.
(*See page* 57)

54. *Vases with inlaid colours and gold, by Poli, Seguso Vetri d'Arte,* 1939.
(*See page* 57)

55A. *Vases in vetro gemmato, by Ercole Barovier,* 1936.
Ht. (*tall vase*) 14 *in.*
(*See page* 57)
55B. *Dishes in vetro rugiada, by Ercole Barovier,* 1940.
Diam. (*large dish*) 18 *in.*
(*See page* 57)

56. *Cut-glass vase, by Murray, Stevens & Williams,* 1939. *Ht.* $8\frac{1}{8}$ *in.*
Victoria and Albert Museum
(*See page* 61)

57A. *Engraved vase, by Murray, Stevens & Williams,* 1932.
Ht. $2\frac{3}{4}$ *in.*
Victoria and Albert Museum
(*See page* 60)

57B. *Engraved vase on a black foot, by Murray, Stevens & Williams,* 1935–40.
Ht. $7\frac{3}{4}$ *in.*
Victoria and Albert Museum
(*See pages* 60, 61)

58A. *'Monart' vase, by Ysart, Moncrieff*, c. 1935. *Ht.* $12\frac{1}{2}$ *in.*
Mr. Norman Sheldon, London
(*See page* 62)

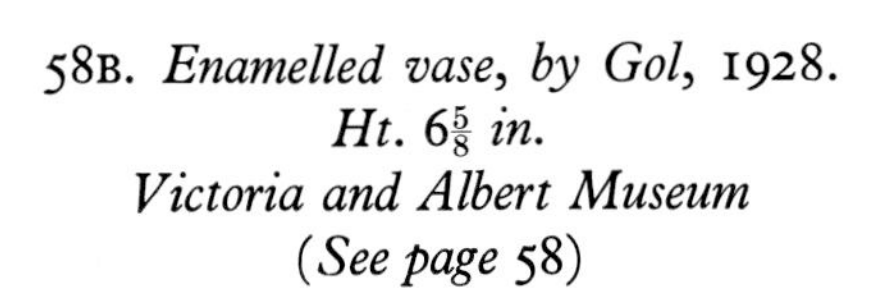

58B. *Enamelled vase, by Gol*, 1928.
Ht. $6\frac{5}{8}$ *in.*
Victoria and Albert Museum
(*See page* 58)

59A. *Vase with cut leaves, by Farquharson, John Walsh Walsh,* 1939. *Ht.* 11¾ *in. Victoria and Albert Museum*
(*See pages* 61, 85)

59B. *Vase of green glass, by Barnaby Powell and Tom Hill, Whitefriars,* 1939. *Ht.* 8⅜ *in. Victoria and Albert Museum*
(*See page* 59)

60A. *Fruit dish, by Marianne Rath, Lobmeyr,* 1925.
(*See page* 63)
60B. *Engraved vase, by Ena Rottenberg, Lobmeyr,* 1925.
(*See page* 64)

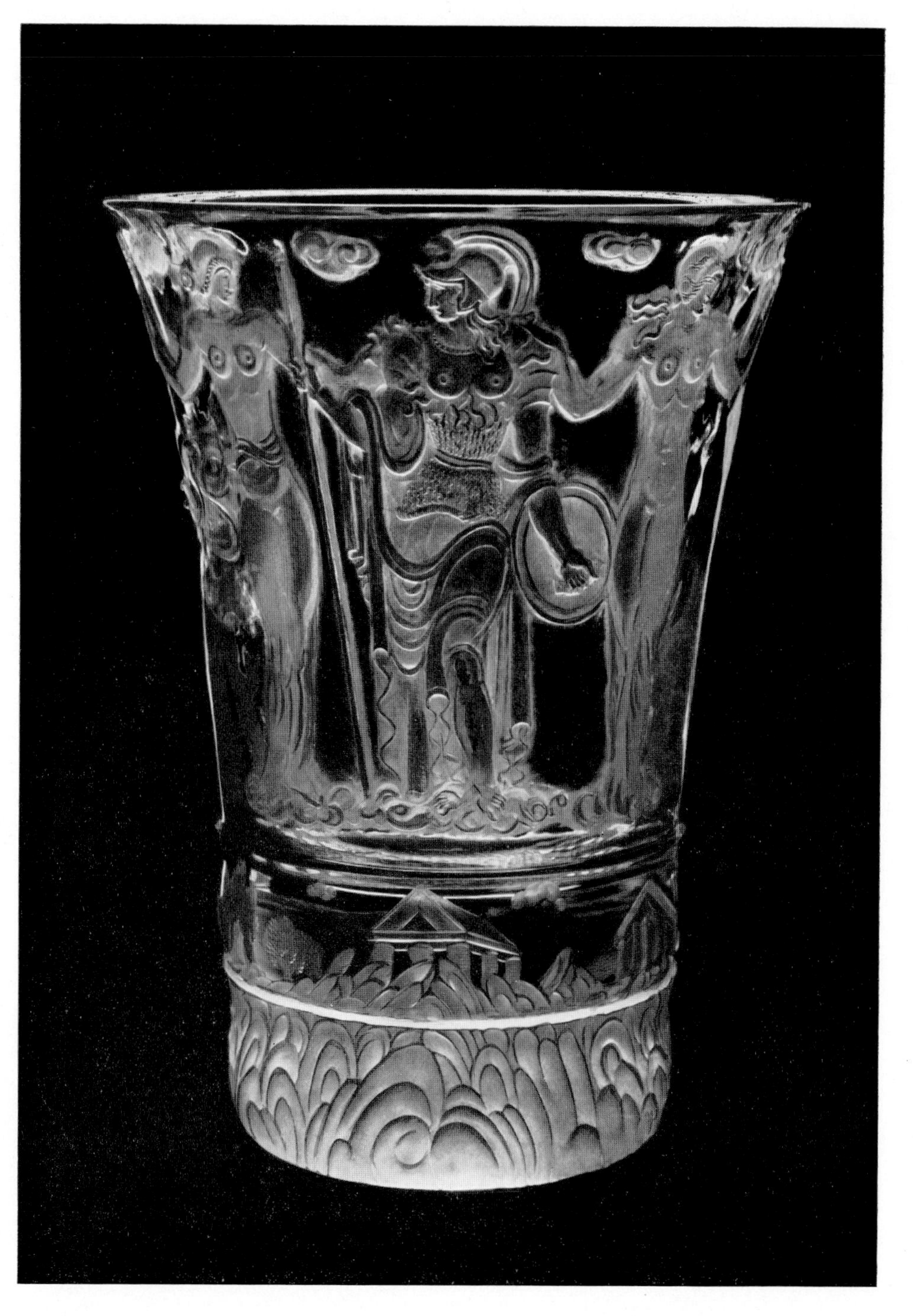

61. *Engraved vase, 'The Three Goddesses', by Horejc, Lobmeyr,* 1925.
(*See page* 63)

62A. *Plaquette in Hochschnitt, by v. Eiff,* 1913. *Ht.* 3⅜ *in. Landesgewerbemuseum, Stuttgart* (*See page* 64)

62B. *Vase with cut decoration, by v. Eiff. Ht.* 12 *in.* (*See page* 64)

63. *Vase with cut decoration, by v. Eiff*, 1935. *Ht.* 11 *in.*
(*See page* 64)

64A. *Vase in vetro pezzato, by Venini. Ht.* $7\frac{1}{2}$ *in.*
Nordenfjeldske Kunstindustrimuseum, Trondheim
(*See page* 67)

64B. *'Folded handkerchief' in latticino, by Venini,* 1940. *Ht.* $11\frac{1}{8}$ *in.*
Victoria and Albert Museum
(*See page* 67)

5A. *Vase in black and yellow vetro* *ssuto, designed by Scarpa for Venini,* 1940.
Ht. 13½ *in.*
Victoria and Albert Museum
(*See page* 67)

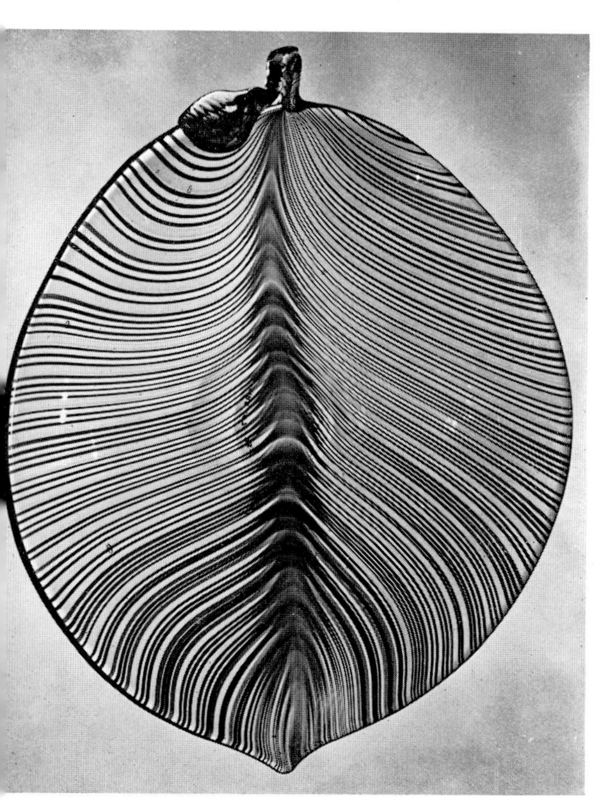

65B. *Dish, designed by Tyra Lundgren for Venini,* 1938.
Length 13½ *in.*
Victoria and Albert Museum
(*See page* 56)

66A. *Vase in green and yellow, by Poli, Seguso Vetri d'Arte,* 1951. *Ht.* 6⅛ *in.*
Victoria and Albert Museum
(*See page* 67)
66B. *Bowl, grey and mauve, by Poli, Seguso Vetri d'Arte,* 1957.
(*See page* 67)

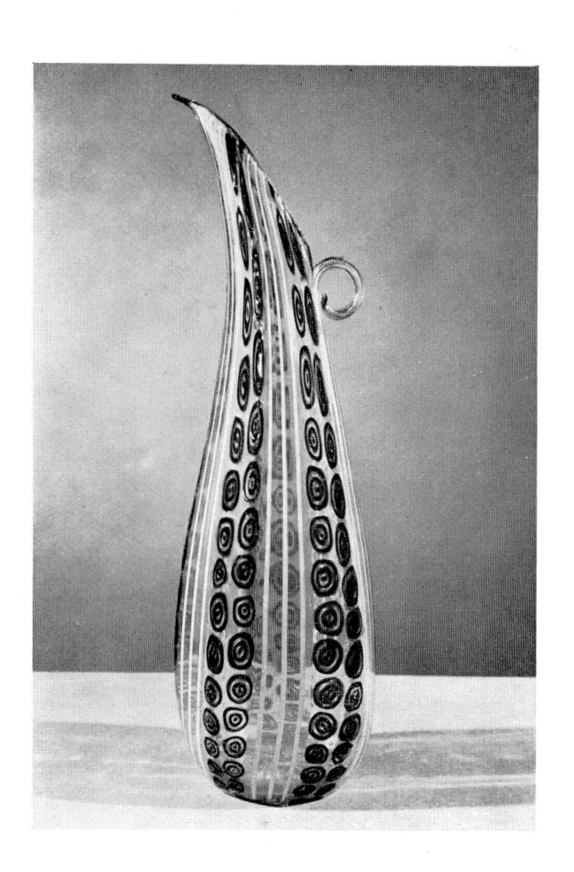

67A. *Jug in vetro damasco, by Ercole Barovier,* 1951. *Ht.* 14 *in.*
67B. *Vases in vetro parabolico, by Ercole Barovier, c.* 1957. *Ht.* 4 *and* 9½ *in.*
Victoria and Albert Museum
(*See page* 67)

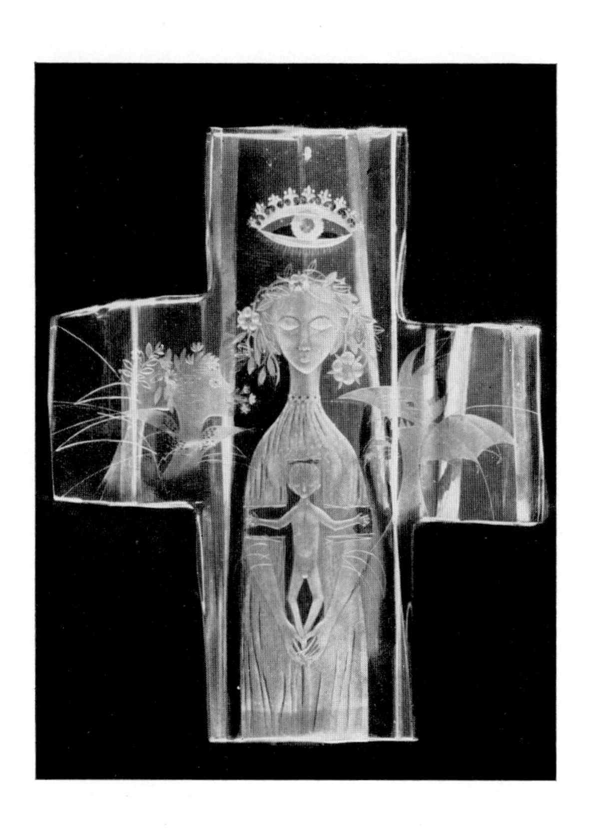

68A. *Engraved cross, by Wirkkala, Karhula-Iittala,* 1951. *Ht.* $17\frac{1}{2}$ *in.* (*See page* 70)
68B. '*Winter*'. *Bowl with wheel- and diamond-engraving, by Åse Voss Schrader,* 1957. (*See page* 73)

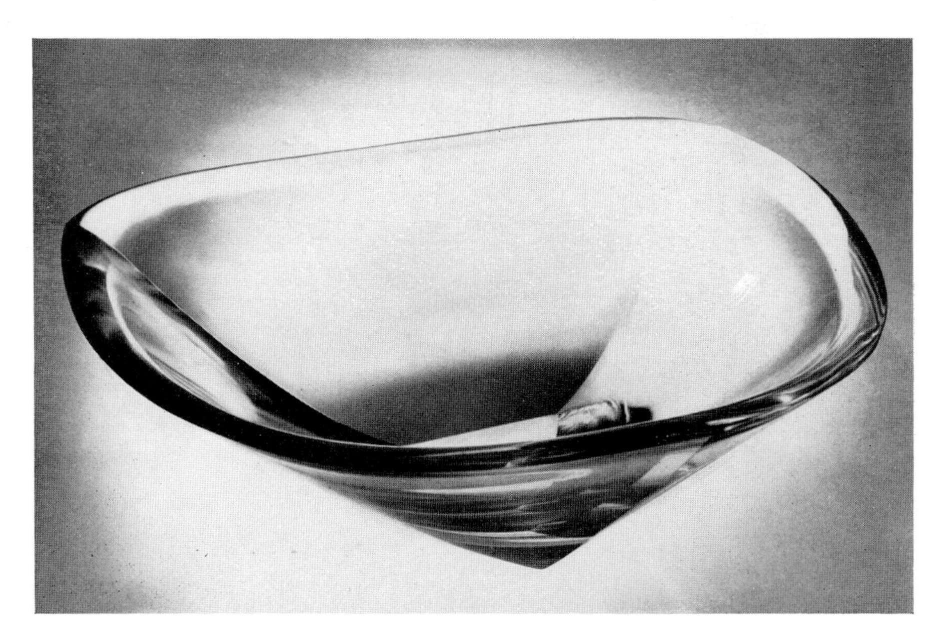

69A. *Folded vase, by Gunnel Nyman,* 1945–47.
(*See page* 69)
69B. *Vase with cut decoration, by Gunnel Nyman,* 1945–47.
(*See page* 69)

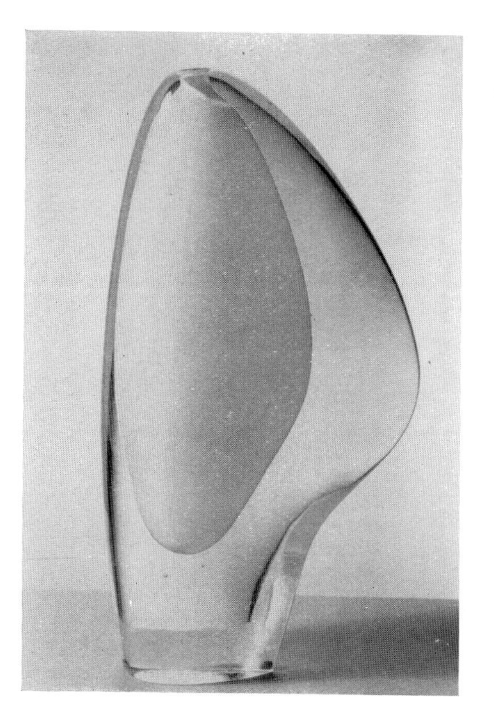

70A. *Vase in clear and opaque white glass, by Sarpaneva, Karhula-Iittala,* 1954. *Ht.* 10 *in.*
Victoria and Albert Museum
(*See page* 70)

70B. *Dish with cut effects, by Wirkkala, Karhula-Iittala,* 1954. *Length* 12¼ *in.*
(*See page* 70)

71A. *Engraved vase, by Wirkkala, Karhula Iittala, 1946. Ht.* $8\frac{1}{4}$ *in. Victoria and Albert Museum*
(*See page* 70)

71B. *Enamelled dish, by Heaton, c.* 1950.
(*See page* 75)

72. *Coloured glass, by Hald, Orrefors, c.* 1956.
(*See page* 70)

73A. *Engraved bottle, by Ingeborg Lundin, Orrefors, 1955.*
(*See page* 71)

73B. *Engraved bowl, by Öhrström, Orrefors, 1954.*
(*See page* 71)

74. *Opal-green vase and vase with black spiral, by Lindstrand, Kosta,* 1956.
(*See page* 71)

75A. *Vase by Gehlin, Gullaskruf*, 1951.
(*See page* 71)

75B. *Engraved vase, by Percy, Gullaskruf*, 1954.
(*See page* 71)

76A. *Bowl in pale-grey glass, by Gerda Strömberg, Strömbergshyttan,* 1940.
Ht. $9\frac{1}{4}$ *in.*
(*See page* 51)
76B. *Bowl with cut animal figure, by Dahlskog, Kosta,* 1926–29.
(*See page* 49)

77A. *Vase by Graffart, Val-Saint-Lambert,* 1950. *Ht.* 8 *in.*
(*See page* 77)
77B. *Vases by Nylund, Strömbergshyttan,* 1957.
(*See page* 72)

78A. *Vase by Jutrem, Hadeland,* 1951. *Ht.* $6\frac{1}{2}$ *in.*
(*See page* 72)

78B. *Vase of green glass, by Jutrem, Hadeland,* 1954. *Ht.* $17\frac{1}{2}$ *in.*
(*See page* 72)

79A. *Vases with coloured inlay, by Bongard, Hadeland, 1954.*
(*See page 72*)

79B. *Bottle with coloured spirals and dots, by Jutrem, Hadeland, 1959. Ht. 10¾ in.*
(*See page 72*)

80A. *Moulded goblets, by Awashima,* 1957. *Ht.* $3\frac{7}{8}$ *and* $4\frac{1}{4}$ *in.*
Victoria and Albert Museum
(*See page* 76)
80B. *Vase by A. D. Copier, Leerdam, c.* 1953.
(*See page* 75)

81A. *Opaque white bowl with black edge, by Meydam, Leerdam, 1952.*
(*See page* 75)
81B. *Sculptural form, by Meydam, Leerdam, 1955.*
(*See page* 75)

82A. *Tricorn bowl, Steuben, c.* 1955. *Diam* 9½ *in.*
(*See page* 75)
82B. *Vase with engraved design by Paul Tchelitchew, Steuben,* 1939. *Ht.* 12½ *in.*
Victoria and Albert Museum (*See pages* 54, 88)

83A. *Plate with engraved design, by Isamu Noguchi, Steuben,* 1955. *Diam.* 10 *in.*
Columbus Gallery of Fine Arts
(*See page* 75)

83B. '*Cathedral*' *by Thompson, Steuben,* 1955. *Ht.* 16 *in.*
(*See page* 75)

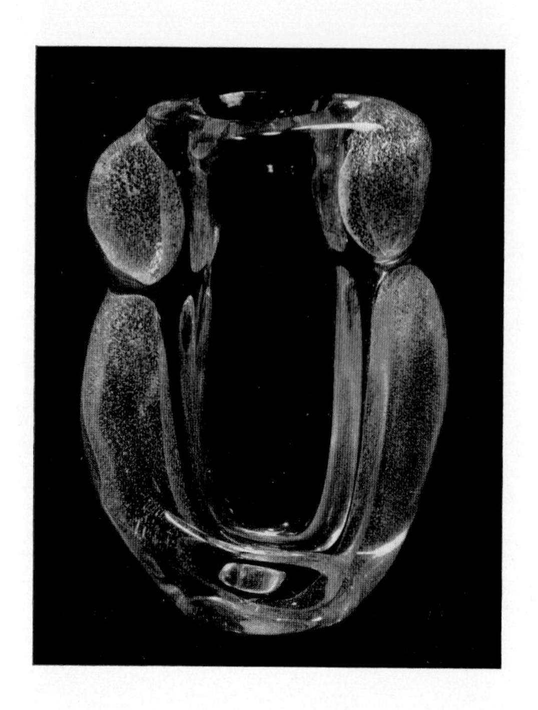

84A. *Vase with details in bubbled glass, by Thuret, c.* 1950. *Ht.* 8 *in.*
(*See page* 76)

84B. *'Le Coq Gaulois', Baccarat,* 1954.
(*See page* 77)

85A. *Vase by Daum, post-war.*
(*See page* 77)
85B. *Abstract form, by Daum, post-war.*
(*See page* 77)

86A. *Vase, by Baxter, Whitefriars, 1957. Ht. 9½ in.*
(*See page* 77)

86B. *Decanter with mauve spirals, by John Richie, Royal College of Art, London,* 1960.
(*See page* 79)

87A. *Sandblasted vase, by Irene M. Stevens, Webb Corbett, c. 1957. Ht. 10⅞ in.*
Victoria and Albert Museum
(*See page* 78)

87B. *Flat bowl with threads and cutting, by Michael Fairbairn.*
Royal College of Art, London, 1960.
(*See page* 79)

88A. *Book-end, by Helen Monro Turner, 1959. Ht. 5½ in. British Glass Industry Research Association, Sheffield*
(*See page* 79)

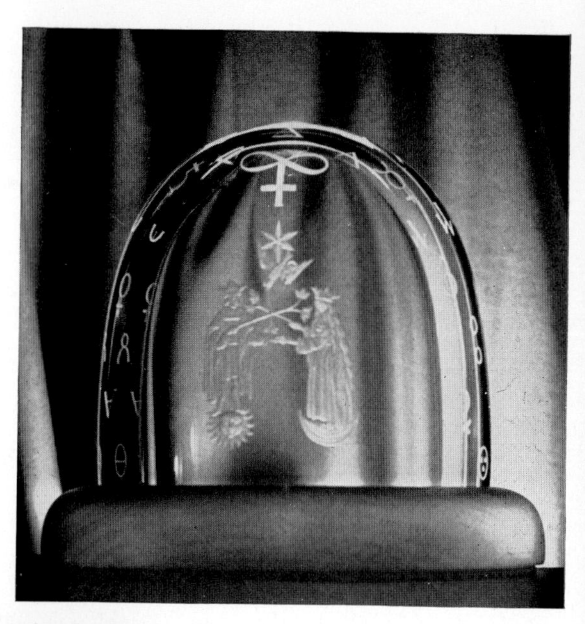

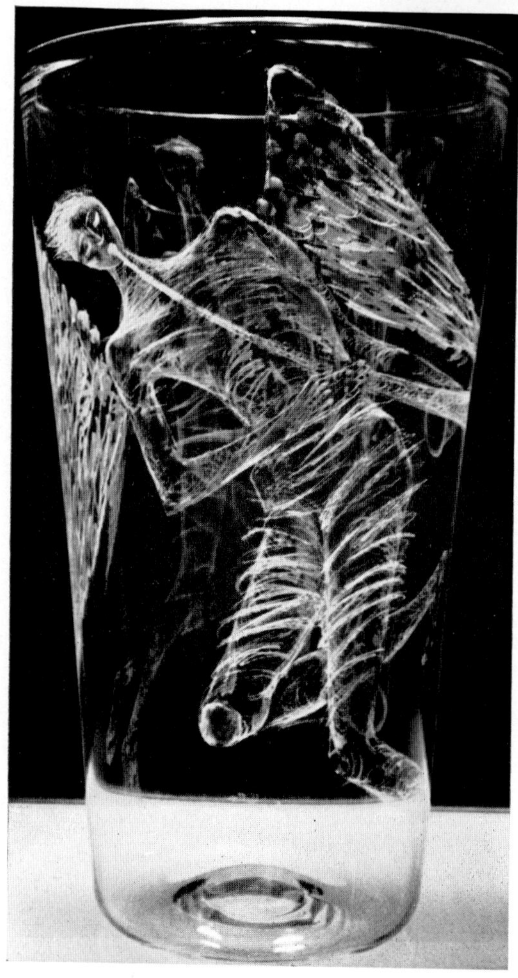

88B. *Vase engraved with angels from Coventry Cathedral, by John Hutton, 1960. Ht. 17½ in. A. Hudson Davis*
(*See page* 80)

89. *'Fireworks', stippled and diamond-engraved glass (detail),*
by Whistler, 1955.
Lady Faber, London
(*See page* 79)

90. *'The Flowers of Bohemia', by Věra Lišková,* 1955.
(*See page* 80)

91. *'Land and Sea'*, *by Horejc, Kamenický Šenov*, 1957.
Ht. 13½ *in.*
(*See page* 80)

92. *Figure of leopard with diamond-point decorations, by Zemek,* 1957.
Ht. $4\frac{1}{2}$ *in.*
(*See page* 81)

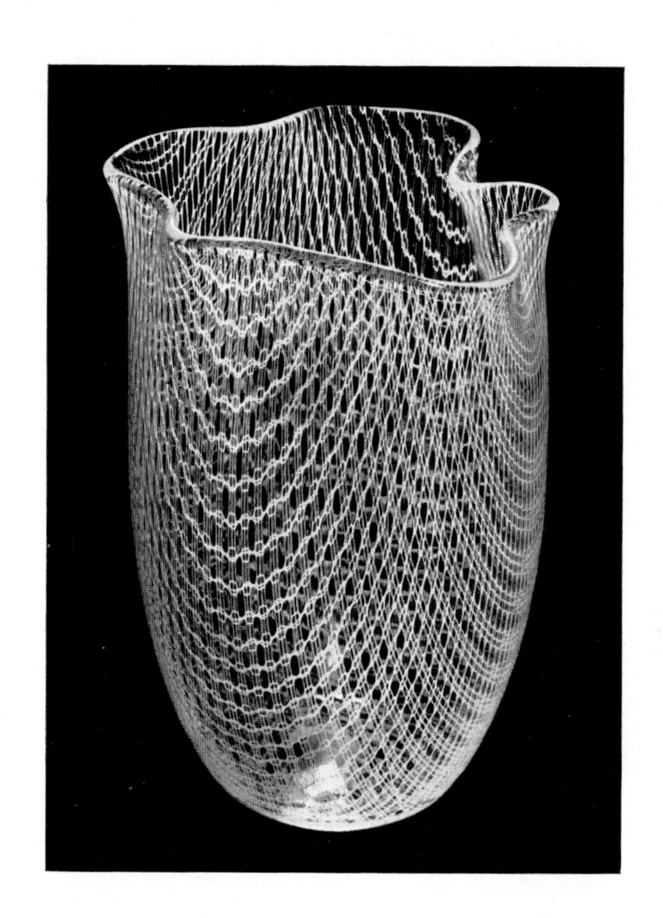

93A. *'Harrtil' glass. Harrachov factory, c.* 1955.
(*See page* 80)
93B. *Bowl by Oldřich Lipa, Prager Kunstgewerbeschule,* 1957.
(*See page* 81)

94A. *Bottle of blue glass, by Bang, Kastrup,* 1956.
(*See page* 73)

94B. *Vases by Lütken, Holmegaard,* 1956.
(*See page* 73)

95. *Vases by Habermeier, Gralglashütte, c.* 1955.
(*See page* 74)

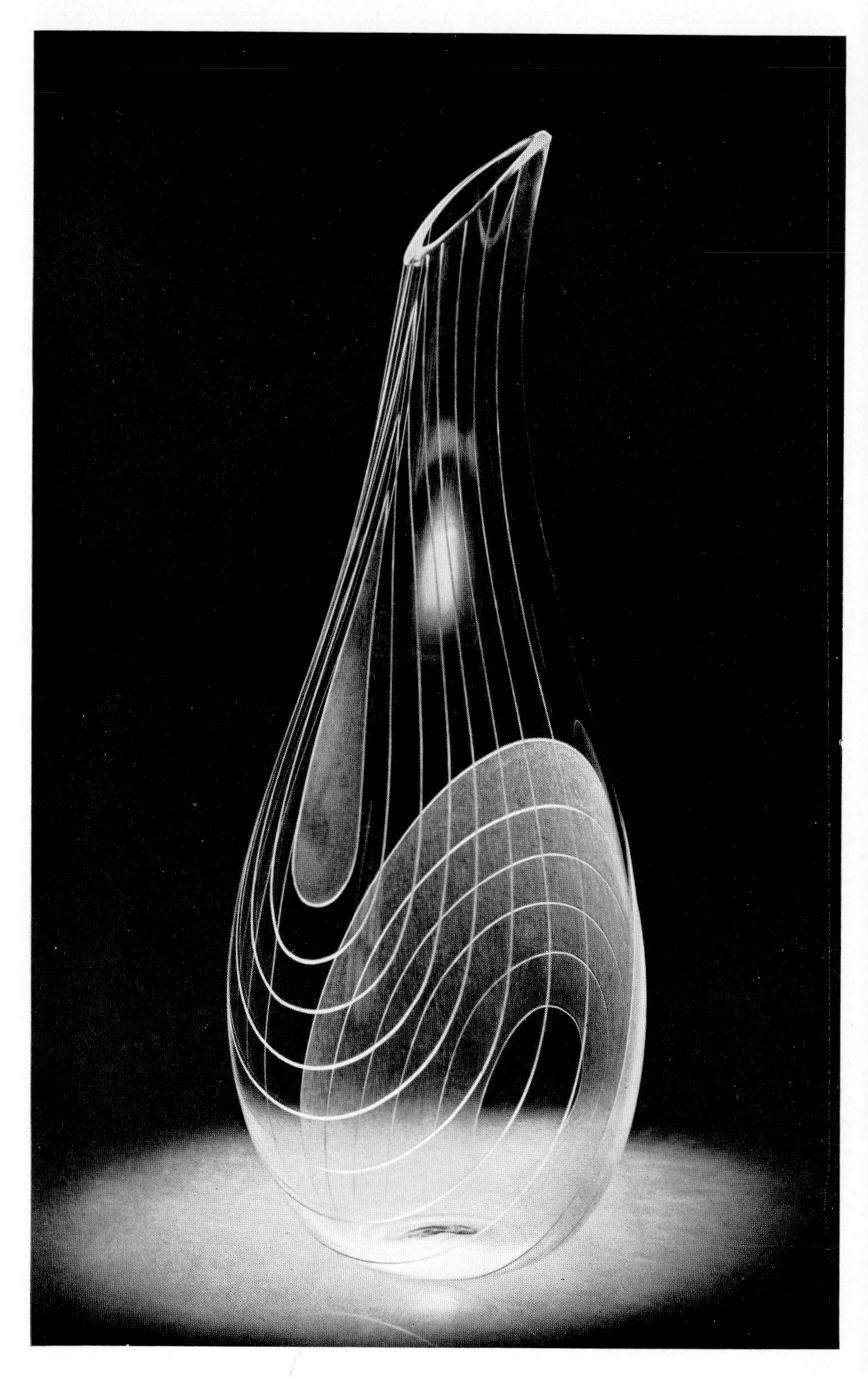

96. *Engraved vase by Habermeier, Gralglashütte,* 1955.
(*See page* 74)